Messages from Heaven

Galia

The moving story of a special child
and her mother who communicate via
Facilitated Communication

Shulamit Gad

ISRAEL BOOKSHOP
LAKEWOOD, NJ

Galia

Messages from Heaven

Distributed by:
Israel Book Shop
501 Prospect Street
Lakewood, N.J. 08701
Tel: 732-901-3009 / Fax: 732-901-4012
Email: isrbkshp@aol.com

Translation from Hebrew: Daniel Makover, (Israel) 03-579 0820
Editing: Rena Joseph
Final Editing: Yael Lock 732-905-0917
Cover Design: DC Design 732-901-4784
Book Layout and Design: Fit to Print 732-367-5273

This work is a translation and compilation
of three books about Galia that were published in Hebrew:

Galia — Messages From Heaven, 437 pages,

Goodbye to Galia? (includes *Messages From Heaven II*), 343
    pages,

Galia — Messages from Heaven, 435 pages (includes the first
    two, with additional new messages

Printed in the United States of America

To My Galia With Love

My dear beloved Galia,

When I asked you what present you wanted for your twelfth birthday, your Bas Mitzva, you told me, "My dear, beloved Ima, the biggest happiness for me is that I am with you. And the book you are writing about me — that is the most wonderful gift you can give me. So hurry up with it, so you can give it to me on time."

You are so special and so unlike others that even the present you want is original. And as you requested, with the help of Heaven, I now present you with the book about you, *baruch Hashem*.

The book is dedicated to you, Galia, my beloved, precious daughter, on the occasion of your twelfth birthday, your Bas Mitzva.

My little Galia, the joy of my life, the happiness of my life, you are the wonderful present which Hashem sent me as part of the kindness He does in this, our world. You succeeded in bringing the spring into my life, the anemones, the chrysanthemums ... the *shefa* of light.

You are my beautiful, beloved princess. Always smiling. Always pleasant, genteel, easygoing, and considerate. You never complain. When you were born, I thought you were one of the 36 hidden *tzadikim*.

My dear beloved Galia, through unlimited sacrifice, stubbornness, resourcefulness, and great love, you got your mother to do *teshuva* and helped her to write a book about you. Galia, thank you so much.

You taught me that "the blessing of a mother has the power to change the fate of her daughter." You said that if a mother is a woman who walks on the path of Hashem — it really helps her children and is the source of all her blessings.

My blessing for you Galia, the only one I love, is that *HaKadosh Baruch Hu* bless you with all the best in life and *shefa*. May He give you joy, happiness, and health until you die at age 120, in serenity and contentment. May your suffering and torment come to an end. May you have the *zechus* to see *Mashiach* quickly, in our days, together with the whole Jewish people, Amen! May you become a regular, normal child, like everyone, able to talk and walk. That will be the fulfillment of my dreams.

Yours in endless love, forever,
Ima

It is clear that I am not qualified to provide letters of recommendation, but since the author, the *tzadekes* and Torah activist, Shulamit Gad, has asked me to, I am not able to refuse.

Thus, I add just the following remark to what other Torah leaders have already noted. What I managed to read in *Galia* (and similarly in *Secrets of the Soul*) shocked me to the depths of my soul.

And since it is clear that the author, Shulamit Gad, wrote the book and is distributing it only for the purpose of spreading Torah, I therefore enthusiastically support buying the book and reading it, and anyone who has the *zechus* to read it, should pass it on to others.

Sincerely yours,
Rabbi Uri Zohar

Today we live in a world in which what a person sees is what he believes. Most people think that what they see is all that exists; if one can't see something, then it doesn't exist. For this reason, they lead materialistic lives and completely ignore the spiritual life. In recent years, the Creator opened the eyes of the blind, i.e., those who think that what a person sees is all that there is to see, through a newly developed technique of communication with the mentally disabled called Facilitated Communication.

Through this method of communication the supremacy of the spiritual over the material is revealed. We see a person who, on the one hand, is terribly deprived on the material level but yet, on the spiritual level, has astonishing powers. This fact, and in particular the messages which the disabled pass on, are able to make many of those sunk in the mire of materialism rethink their lives and face the truth. It is therefore a great and important *mitzva* to publicize the messages from these people, who by their own testimony live in the world of truth and whose messages come from the upper worlds.

Indeed through a meticulous check of the messages written by the mentally disabled, we find that they correspond amazingly with texts in classic religious works, despite the fact that these people have never studied these texts. The fact that they write out things found in various texts written by our great scholars, and that those who help them to write, called facilitators, are completely unfamiliar with these topics, is a proof that we live in a world where what the eye sees is but a small fraction of what actually exists. This is evidenced from the fact that we are confronted with children suffering from mental incompetence, appearing to be severely retarded, who have never learned to read or write and who never studied religious literature — who reveal themselves as great experts in the field. Where do they get this vast knowledge and how do they succeed in expressing themselves with such richness of language, style and content? Is this not proof of the limits of our powers of perception?

Galia, a girl who suffers from severe mental incompetence, is classified as being totally incapacitated. Through FC, her extremely rich spiritual world has been revealed. She has succeeded in bringing her mother to do *teshuva*, raising her from the "the deep pit to the lofty heights." Not only has she succeeded in removing her from the world of falsity to the world of truth, but she has also made her mother into a public campaigner for the cause of Torah, dedicated to waking up those who are sleeping and who walk in darkness, in order to bring them back to their Father in Heaven. Blessed are those public advocates who are fortunate both in this world and the next world.

Therefore I fully recommend to every Jew, even those who are "in the light" and tread upon the path of truth, to carefully and attentively read the significant messages of Galia that are now being made available to the public in this important book. These messages are able to inspire all of us, each at his own level. Particularly in these tumultuous times, we need special guidance in order to focus our attention on rectifying various spiritual failings. This will, in turn, enable the individual and the nation as a whole to get through the difficult days preceding the arrival of *Mashiach*, in peace.

Concerned for the ailing spiritual condition of the nation and awaiting its merciful salvation,

Rabbi Yehuda Srevnik
(Author of "Secrets of the Soul")

COMMENTS OF
HaGaon Rav Aharon Leib Steinman *Shlita*
Regarding Facilitated Communication

In comments to Rabbi Yehuda Srevnik regarding Facilitated Communication, Rav Steinman stated (and he authorized Rabbi Srevnik to quote this in his name in "Secrets of the Soul") that he sees in this phenomenon the great mercy of Heaven to wake up the sleeping who forget the truth amid the ephemeralities of routine life, and abuse their whole life with empty pursuits and indulgences. It is also a source of moral inspiration for the Torah community, who today are also in need of strengthening. The statements of the mentally incompetent are fiery *mussar* and stir all those who read them to the path of *teshuva*. It is a worthy cause to disseminate and publicize these statements.

Rav Steinman has personally attended communication sessions with the mentally incompetent and was very impressed by the answers that they gave to his questions.

In Rav Steinman's opinion, it is very important to contemplate these messages and search one's soul. One should not disregard the messages.

He also warned that one should not use the statements of the mentally incompetent for any specific purpose or *halachic* ruling, and one must not ask them about the future.

"We have had the *zechus* of the discovery of this phenomenon for one purpose only: to bring the hearts of the Jewish people closer to their Father in Heaven."

COMMENTS OF
RABBI NOSSON M. WACHTFOGEL ZT"L
REGARDING FACILITATED COMMUNICATION

"The people who walk in darkness saw great light." We are living in a period of great darkness and confusion. Many of our people are not even aware of their Father in Heaven, and even amongst those who walk on the path of truth, some are still far from perfection.

The Creator has compassion on his people and, in His great mercy, has sent us something capable of waking people up from their deep slumber, namely a new form of communication with the mentally incompetent.

Through this form of communication we see that the spiritual world is revealed to them. Despite the fact that the world regards them as devoid of understanding and awareness of what is going on around them, by means of this new form of communication, which is called Facilitated Communication, we discover that their knowledge of the spiritual affairs of the world, of the Creator, of ethics and of morals, are on a very high level. This fact has already inspired many Jews to return to their roots or to heighten their devotion to Torah and *mitzvos*.

Due to my many commitments, I was unable to read through this book and asked a *talmid chacham*, whom I trust implicitly, to review it. He indeed reviewed a large part of the book and conveyed its contents to me. In addition, his first hand observations of this form of communication caused him to conclude that it is authentic and highly valuable.

At the same time, it must be stressed that while the messages conveyed by the mentally incompetent are suitable for strengthening and bringing people closer to the truth, a person should not act upon what they say without referring to a Rabbi. For as is known, only Torah sages may guide our nation.

I would like to bless all those who seek to publicize these important messages for the purpose of sanctifying the name of Heaven and magnifying His name in the world. May Hashem help them succeed in their endeavors.

Rabbi Nosson Wachtfogel

[Many] of the mentally disabled individuals in Israel, communicating through Facilitated Communication, have expressed their wish that those of their statements which compare with passages from source texts be published with the appropriate references from the Bible, the Talmud and other works. I feel that doing this will provide great inspiration since it shows how their pronouncements are anchored and rooted in our holy sources. The sources for their statements that I found show us that we cannot ignore what they say.

For thousands of years, sufferers from autism, Down's syndrome and cerebral palsy were thought of as "imbeciles." Now we have discovered that they are of sound, clear mind and capable of expressing themselves — by means of communication — on a level far above ours. For many, this is not easy to accept. But this does not change the fact that it is true, as it has been proved beyond a doubt on many occasions.

Finally, two outstanding Talmudic scholars passed on this manuscript [Rabbi Krausz's] to one of the Torah sages of our time on my behalf. He warmly and heartily approved its publication and said it is a *tikun* for their souls; and that it will be a great *zechus* for us, if it inspires us to do *teshuva*.

The same sage warned against possible mishaps linked to FC. We must listen to his warning that one should not ask them questions which can lead to making decisions, for example in matters of *halacha* and medical affairs, since they do not serve as a substitute for sages, rabbis and doctors.

Sincerely,
Rabbi Gavriel Krausz

Acknowledgments

Praise and thanks to *HaKadosh Baruch Hu* for all of Your kindness and wonders. For giving me my Galia; for the great *zechus* of my becoming religious; for enabling me to communicate with Galia and to publish her messages; for allowing me to participate in the movement to spread Torah; and for all of the help which I was privileged to receive from Heaven.

My thanks and blessings to the following rabbis, *shlita,* for their approval, recommendations and help in my attempt to help spread Torah:

Rabbi Yehuda Srevnik *shlita*, **Rabbi Yisrael Lugasi** *shlita,* and **Rabbi Uri Zohar** *shlita* for their letters of recommendation for the three books on Galia, *Galia — Messages From Heaven* I, II and III;

Rabbi Menachem Grilack, editor of religious books and magazines, for reading and checking the manuscript of the first book on Galia;

R' Reuven Salman for his help in editing the second book on Galia;

R' Daniel Makover for translating the book into English;

Rabbi Yechiel Sitzman for all of his advice;

Rena Joseph for editing the English version of this book;

And to all my colleagues, known and unknown to me, in the *kiruv* movement, striving to bring our brothers and sisters of the House of Israel back to our Father in Heaven.

May the *zechus* of this book contribute:

To the peaceful redemption of the Jewish people, the revelation of *Mashiach*, and the construction of the *Beis Hamikdash* in our time;

To the complete cure of all of the sick of our nation so that we all may serve *Hashem* in health and strength;

To the benefit of the souls of:

My father, Avraham the son of Simcha Ben Ezra *z"l*;

My grandfather, Yosef Cohen *z"l*;

My beloved mother, Miriam the daughter of Chaninah Ben Ezra Cohen *z"l*;

My sister, Deborah the daughter of Miriam *z"l*;

My grandmother, Chaninah Cohen *z"l*;

All the members of my family who have passed on.

May their righteous souls rest in *Gan Eden* and be a shield to protect me and my children and my family and all of the Jewish people.

A personal prayer:

Hashem, may it be your will: that You give me, my children and family and Your people, the Jewish nation, the *zechus* to return to *Hashem* with our entire hearts quickly; to fulfill Your *mitzvos* and study Torah with genuine motivation, for Your sake; and may all of our actions be for the sake of Heaven. Grant us a good income, enabling us to live in conditions of comfort. Give us healthy minds and healthy bodies. Save us from all distress, pain, the *yetzer hora,* and forbidden thoughts. Give all of us happiness, serenity, peace, relief and success in all that we do and make all of our desires come true, if they are for our true benefit. Amen! May this be Your will!

Shulamit Gad
Cholon, Israel

Table of Contents

Introduction

This book gives the reader messages from the world of truth! — The astonishing messages of Galia, a child who suffers from mental incompetence, 100% physical disability, and serious mental retardation. Today she is fifteen and a half years old and communicates with her mother (an academic teacher of many years with the Ministry of Education in Israel) by means of an amazing communication method that was discovered recently in various places in the world, called Facilitated Communication or FC. This is a relatively new and exciting alternative method of communication, enabling the mentally disabled to convey words and thoughts. Galia's introduction to this form of communication will be described in *Part I: "Facilitated Communication and My Galia."*

✺ *What is FC?*

Facilitated Communication, or FC, is an alternative method of communication meant to help people with mental incompetence. This method successfully assists children and adults of all ages with language and speech difficulty. Participants are generally unable to communicate due to autism, Down's Syndrome, Rett's, cerebral palsy, or a comatose condition.

Non-verbal people with mental incompetence, or who are very limited in their use of words, can convey their thoughts and desires through FC by pointing at an alphabet board or by typing on a home or portable computer.

The individual with the disability pushes his or her hand to the alphabet board and points at the letters on the board. By combining letters, words are spelled out, and this leads to sentences. Throughout the world, people with mental incompetence write in this way. By pointing at letters or typing on a keyboard, brain-damaged people (of all ages) write poems and articles on many varied subjects, learn math and biology, order a meal at a restaurant, or shop at a convenience store.

In most cases, the facilitator gives the person hand support by holding or steadying the back of the hand, the palm or forearm; for this reason the technique is called "Facilitated Communication."

Over the course of time, it is possible to reduce the amount of support some individuals receive. Some FC users overcome the need for physical support and manage with the facilitator just standing beside them or touching their shoulder, head, hand or garment. There are some who are able to communicate without any need for hand support or any other kind of support at all. All of this has been documented and has been captured on films that have been shown throughout the world. This will be elaborated upon in *Part I, Chapter Two* and *Chapter Three.*

✢ *The Spiritual Component*

In Israel and throughout the world, people with mental incompetence, aside from communicating everyday messages, write out extraordinary spiritual messages and deep insights into Torah that are beyond the abilities of many facilitators to comprehend. They also study Torah with advanced students in a special yeshiva for students with autism, and author original, in-depth insights.

Communications of deep spiritual messages occur mostly to Jewish children from Torah-observant homes, although two books have been published in the United States that also contain spiritual messages: *A Child Of Eternity* (by Kristi Jorde, mother of a mentally incompetent child) and *Memoirs Of An Autistic Child* (John Chambers).

Another book recently published in France, *I Choose Your Hand To Talk*, is written by a speech therapist, Anne-Marguerite Vexiau. She discusses telepathy and other supernatural issues in FC communication.

By means of Facilitated Communication, children who are otherwise completely uncommunicable and detached from their surroundings tell of their past lives in this world, describe the existence of a spiritual world after death, and attest to the fact that G-d exists and that the individual is responsible for his actions.

In *A Child Of Eternity*, the child tells her mother that one of her purposes in coming to this world is to influence people to love G-d. She also writes of the importance of loving one's fellow man.

Galia's spiritual messages will be presented in *Part II* and *Part III. Part III, Chapter Ten: "Galia and Her Ima,"* contains poignant personal communications between Galia and her mother, and illustrates the strong bond that developed between them as a result of Facilitated Communication. Many very interesting messages, some of which are lengthy, or did not belong in other chapters, are collected in *Part III, Chapter Thirteen: "Ends and Beginnings, The Conversations Continue."*

It is important to note the following points, which have been clarified by our Torah leaders as well as by the children themselves:

1. Although the souls of those with mental dysfunction know everything without material and temporal limitations, one must not forget that their bodies are extremely restricted and they require our help for their daily needs. Giving them this help enables the body, which serves as a receptacle for the soul, to protect the precious deposit placed within it and return it to the Creator at the proper time.

2. It is forbidden to communicate with people with mental incompetence and autism without the written consent of their parents. Failure to comply can involve criminal proceedings.

3. It is forbidden to hold communication sessions with the mentally incompetent on a stage in front of an audience or to make communication into any kind of entertainment show.

4. Any communication session should be conducted with the utmost discretion, in privacy and seclusion, calmly and pleasantly, without a gathering of onlookers and with all the respect due to any person.

5. A recognized and known rabbi must check all messages before they are publicized to prevent passing on any distortion of Torah, *chas vechalila.*

6. Mentally incompetent people who see the truth and the spiritual worlds without distraction, and hear the *bas kol* of Heaven announcing what is about to take place in our world, pass on only what Heaven allows them to convey. Their dire predictions are not bound to take place. In Heaven, everything is dynamic and can change in a moment. And with Torah, *mitzvos*, prayer, honesty, decency, helping others, and our other *maasim tovim*, the *kitrugim* and *gezairos* against us will be canceled *be-ezras Hashem* and *HaKadosh Baruch Hu* will dispense only happy *gezairos*. Amen.

Part 1

Facilitated Communication and My Galia

To My Dear Galia with love,

When you were born, I thought your terrible condition was a blow that would ruin my life. But Hashem in His mercy has shown me, my Galia, that you are the most wonderful gift I have ever received in my life. Thank you to the Creator of the World for giving me Galia. I have always loved you without limit, my little darling.

It was so difficult to cope, accept and reconcile myself to the fact that you weren't like all girls, because you were so different and special. The penetrating glances always thrown at us from all directions, all the running around to seek out the proper medical treatments, your brothers who suffered so much in their struggle to come to terms with your condition — how difficult it all was. We envied you, thinking that you didn't know how painful it is to be mentally incompetent, and how much pain that caused all of us. We didn't grasp the greatness of your suffering and understanding. This took years.

Galia, my beloved, you gave us a big surprise when it was discovered that it was possible to communicate with you through an alphabet board. You shocked us when you pushed your hand, pointed at letters and revealed the words of Hashem to me.

You became my best friend in this world. You brought a whole range of colors into my life. No moment can compare with the happy moment in which I discovered you, Galia, a clever, understanding child who knew everything.

My amazing child. My whole life changed beyond recognition. You enriched my life with a wealth of happiness and light. You are my tzadekes. You have fulfilled your mission faithfully, with unlimited self-sacrifice. With love and patience, you got me, a mother as old as I am, to do teshuva. You gave me tremendous guidance and taught me an enormous amount. A great zechus fell to my lot to share my life with you, my dear tzadekes. A great zechus has also fallen to the lot of our generation to receive your messages from the higher worlds.

My Galia, you have strengthened scores of people and inspired them to return to our Father in Heaven, who loves us, His beloved sons and daughters. Thousands have the read the Hebrew book, Galia — Messages from Heaven, and were shocked by the important messages which you passed on to us from Heaven. Because of you, Galia, thousands are opening their eyes to see the truth coming down to the world.

Your Loving Ima

Chapter One:

My Personal Story

**The letters of Galia (גליה)
can also spell out Gila(גילה),
which means joy!**

Chapter One

My name is Shulamit. I am a senior teacher working in the area of special education with the Israeli Ministry of Education. I was formerly a kindergarten teacher. I received a B.A. at Bar Ilan University in Education and Criminology and studied toward an M.A. in Education at the School of Education at Hebrew University.

I was completely non-religious, totally alienated from anything having to do with Torah and *mitzvos*. I did a full tour of duty in the army, serving as a sergeant in the teachers unit of the Southern Command. I am the mother of three children — two grown sons and Galia, who is now fifteen and a half. Needless to say, I was thrilled when Galia was born after two boys. I envisioned dressing her up in pretty dresses, tying her hair in ponytails and ribbons, and going for enjoyable and pleasant walks with her.

But my sweet dream came to an early end. Galia hardly developed. She remained a little baby. Today, at fifteen and a half years of age, she functions mentally and physically like a baby of four or five months old — in all respects. She cannot speak a single word. She cannot stand up. She is still in diapers and eats only baby food. And if that's not enough, she also has three congenital heart defects. Galia's diagnosis describes her as mentally disabled, severely retarded and physically handicapped.

ᢧ The Turnaround

These troubles came to light shortly after she was born, and I felt overcome with the feeling that my life was ruined, its balance lost. When I became Torah observant, I realized *baruch Hashem* that Galia was sent by Heaven to save me in this world and the next. But until then I believed that having to look after Galia in her state was no less than a terrible blow. Now I know that you have to take all the knocks lovingly because they are just the smacks of a loving father. Our Father in Heaven in His goodness and mercy loves us, but sometimes strikes us, his beloved sons and daughters, to wake us up, to make us open our eyes, and to save us from the danger hovering above us. He is like a loving mother who occasionally punishes her child in order to teach him and to warn him to stay away from danger. The little boy doesn't understand why. He has not yet developed the faculties for understanding his situation.

The blow I got with the birth of Galia created a complete turnaround in the way I thought. My life was totally reformatted in an entirely new mode. My eyes opened up. The blow got me to start thinking about what was going on around me. This would not have occurred had not Galia come to the world in such a terrible plight, so restricted and so helpless. That blow is what got me to do *teshuva*. The blow became the best present I ever got in my life. Hashem in His great mercy and kindness gave me this blow to open my eyes, to bring me out from the darkness I was living in and to see all the pieces of the mixed-up puzzle suddenly fitting together to form a complete and clear picture. A picture of beautiful perfection.

A friend once told me that Galia's suffering in this world serves no purpose and that her life here is completely superfluous. It was clear to me that she said this due to a lack of understanding and a spiritual and emotional insensitivity. It's obvious that every soul is sent to our world by Heaven to fulfill an extremely important mission — a specific mission that only it and no other soul can fulfill.

Galia was sent to our world for the fulfillment of a grand mission. Galia brought her mother to do *teshuva*. Because of Galia and the talks I give about her, and because of my radio broadcasts, I feel that the *teshuva* movement here in Israel has gained a great deal.

We live in a world of falsity. In Hebrew, "world" — *olam* — can also mean "hidden." The world hides the truth. We have been given a task to make an effort, to go to the trouble, to search and reflect until the truth is discovered. In fact the truth is never too far off. We just have to look, to stretch out our arms and reach for it.

✣ *The Early Years*

As soon as Galia was born, we had to look after her. Our time was taken up by doctors, doctors and more doctors. We found ourselves going from one to another — professors, department heads, and consultants. Sometimes Galia would have convulsions and contractions and pass out. This required us to go with her to the hospital by ambulance. This would be followed with more treatments, hospitalization and more supervision. One world-famous doctor told us that Galia was "an accident of nature" and that after an accident, you just have to carry on.

We went through treatment after treatment, full of expectations and hope. Every day of the week was filled with therapy sessions — physiotherapy, occupational therapy, and speech therapy. Galia was subjected to constant treatments and follow-ups in numerous outpatient clinics: the child development clinic, the eye clinic, the ear clinic, the genetics department, the neurology department, and the cardiovascular department.

Despite all the medical examinations, to this day the doctors do not know how to explain what caused our Galia's awful condition. They cannot point to the cause or identify the syndrome. What is clear beyond all doubt is that Galia has serious brain incapacity. She has a one hundred percent disability and she will remain in this pitiful plight all her life. Extraordinarily, all the tests Galia went through showed sound results: chromosomes, acids, reflexes, muscles — have all come up normal. Even the CT brain scan was normal. Apart from Galia herself, everything was normal!

❧ *The Endless Marathon*

During the endless marathon of doctors and treatments, my marriage went on the rocks and my husband and I got divorced. The burden was more than I could bear. I decided, with no other option and a broken heart, to stop pondering and place Galia in a good home.

Now began a new marathon — the search for a suitable home. In every home for the mentally incompetent and severely handicapped I visited, I was dismayed to see the terrible neglect of the premises and the horrible attitude toward the residents. The very thought of removing my beloved little Galia — my hopeless baby, my defenseless child — from the house was unbearable, all the more so if it would be to one of these homes. My heart was torn to pieces and I cried tears of anguish.

One of the reasonable suggestions that came up was a nunnery where the nuns devote their lives to looking after the unfortunate and incapacitated. But despite the fact that I was very far from Judaism, I couldn't reconcile myself to the idea that my daughter would be living in a nunnery. The very thought made me shudder.

Fortunately, the solution was not long in coming. In Israel's central area, the religious community had opened up a home for children suffering from serious mental disability. The administrators, caregivers, and staff gave us a warm welcome. People devoted to kindness looked after these poor children with supreme commitment and respect. The institution was a magnificent example of the best that Israeli society had to offer.

Galia was accepted to this wonderful home at the age of six and a half. At last, I could start to sleep at night. I went to visit her a great deal, carried on loving her as much as ever, and continued to tend to her needs as much as possible. Galia always radiated with happiness when I came to visit her. She would hug me and place her wizened arms around my neck with all her might. We would sit in silence, hugging each other — a mother and her daughter sharing love without words.

I finally felt that my luck had improved. I thought about parents who abandon their unfortunate children in institutions and "forget" about them forever. These parents, immediately following childbirth, give up on their brain-damaged children, not having the emotional strength to face their challenge, and so are doomed to spend their entire life mourning over the normal child they had longed for but not received. I did not blame them. I shared their pain.

✥ Discovering FC – Rabbi Srevnik's Lecture

One evening, I happened to hear about a talk on the subject of communicating with autistic people. The lecture was to take place in a public hall called *Mofet* — "Wonder" — in Kiryat Ono.

I attended, expecting to hear from a medical expert. To my surprise, the lecturer was a bearded rabbi from Jerusalem, Rabbi Yehuda Srevnik. This lecture was to cause a complete turnaround in me. You never know how and when you will be confronted with the catalyst that will change your entire life.

I turned up at the talk totally irreligious. I had tousled hair and wore white pants. Modesty in dress or grooming was not even a consideration for me then.

Rabbi Srevnik talked about how it is possible to communicate with autistic and brain damaged persons using a new method of communication called Facilitated Communication. Through FC, people with mental incompetence and autism point at an alphabet board and write extraordinary messages. Among other things, he said that these people claim that this is not their first time on earth. They can tell you who they were in their previous incarnation, about the next world, and the Heavenly Court. They can tell you about *Gan Eden* and *Gehinom*.

The lecture was augmented by videos showing proof of this phenomenon. An American film was projected on a large screen that showed American children communicating through FC. Some of them had become gifted students, studying math, biology, composing poems, articles, etc.

At the end of the riveting talk, I went up to the Rabbi. I told him about my Galia and asked him if I, too, could "talk" with my brain-damaged daughter. He answered affirmatively and gave me the telephone number of an American woman who had studied FC in the States, and had since immigrated to Israel. I called the facilitator at my first opportunity and we arranged a time to have an FC session with Galia. The facilitator did not know me, nor had I ever met or heard of her before.

✵ *Our First Communication Session*

The prospect of communicating with Galia gave me no rest. With great excitement, I tried to imagine myself communicating with her. What I was going to say to my daughter after ten years of total silence? By this time Galia was ten years old, and this would be my first opportunity to communicate with her.

I began preparing for the session by writing down a list of questions such as:

Why did you come to this world in this condition?
What can I do for you?

Of course, there were many other questions as well.

At the top of the page, I wrote down:

Galia, I love you!

It was imperative for me to tell her that I loved her.

The day of the session arrived. The facilitator showed up with a spelling board containing the letters of the alphabet. She put the board on the table in front of Galia, took Galia's hand in hers, clutching all her fingers with the exception of her index finger and asked Galia, "Do you want to write?" Immediately Galia started to push her hand and point at the letters, one after the other. First she spelled out: "Y-E-S!" and then immediately after that she spelled out: "I- M- A, — I- L-O-V-E -Y-O-U."

I burst into tears.

Then, before I asked Galia anything, and even before I had taken the question sheet I had written from my bag, something astonishing occurred. Galia wrote out answers to all the questions that I had prepared on the sheet. Her answers were in the same order as the questions I had written. She pointed at the letters on the alphabet board and wrote: "Ima, I am the soul of your grandmother, Simcha, who died. Heaven sent me to this world to rectify a sin in child rearing. You have *zechus avos* and Heaven has sent me to get you to do *teshuva*."

I was overtaken by shock. I cried. I trembled. The emotion brought on dizziness. I almost fainted.

From the first moment, I knew that Galia's messages were authentic. From that very beginning, it was clear to me that it was Galia who was spelling all this out and not the facilitator. There was no chance that the facilitator knew my grandmother,

Simcha, who died before I was born. There was no chance that the facilitator knew the questions I had prepared or the exact sequence in which they were written. Even my two sons did not know the name of my grandmother, Simcha.

I asked Galia, "Do people have to come back to this world for a sin which seems so insignificant to me, a sin in the way you bring up your children?"

Galia answered, "It's not easy for *tzadikim*."
"You're a *tzadekes*?" I asked naively.
Galia wrote: "I'm a *tzadekes*."
I asked, "What can I do for you? How can I help you?"
Galia answered, "Physically, you can't help me at all. But spiritually, you can do a lot. Your doing *teshuva* helps me. You are my *tikun*."

☙ *The Revolution of My Life*

I started to do *teshuva* with dizzying speed. In less than a month, I had covered my hair and was regularly attending classes in a Torah seminary. Hashem helped me to do *teshuva* quickly. Praise and thanks to the Creator of the World for the *zechus* which was given to me, and for Galia, whom He sent to me in His goodness, to get me to do *teshuva* and to reveal the word of the living G-d, the truth and the light.

Communicating with Galia changed my whole life. It turned me into a calm and happy person. It helped Galia to be a more serene child, and after we began communicating via FC, Galia stopped her continuous crying. My whole approach to Galia also changed. Until then, I had thought that Galia did not understand anything and that it made no difference to her whether she spent her time in my home or the care center. Until then, it was enough for me to visit her in the care center. Once we started communicating, I made a point of taking Galia home every *Shabbos* and for each holiday. My relationship with her deepened along with the deepening of our communication. Our love for each other grew and has since become so strong that today I am often overcome with deep yearnings to rush and see Galia. All this was not the case before we were able to communicate. FC changed our entire relationship for the better.

✺ *I Want To Go Home!*

The first time I took Galia home was after she had been in the care center for many years. I took her home because of one of our early communication sessions. One day the facilitator asked Galia: "Do you want to say something to your Ima?" Galia pointed at the spelling board and wrote, "Tell her to take me with her. It's really hard for me without Ima. I want to go home with her." That day, I took her home for a visit, and since that time I take her home regularly. We pass the time together in happiness and joy. How amazing to be with my great, wonderful daughter, my Galia, who reveals messages from Heaven to me.

Within a few months of our first communication session, I learned, with the help of a facilitator, how to communicate with Galia on my own. This gave me fantastic happiness. I am reminded of the reaction of Professor Schawlow, winner of the Nobel Prize for Physics, who was one of the discoverers of FC with his autistic son, Artie. When he was asked what the happiest moment of his life was, he replied, "The happiest moment of my life was the moment when I succeeded in communicating with my son, Artie — greater than the moment of receiving the Nobel Prize." I felt that I had received far more than the Nobel Prize, I had discovered my daughter.

✺ *The Beauty Of Communication*

Since that time I have been conducting sessions with Galia, who is now fifteen and a half years of age. Galia is truly a source of constant encouragement, strength, and advice. Among other things, Galia has written out messages of extraordinary beauty and depth that have brought me to study the Torah later in life. If not for Galia, I would never have done so.

One of the decisive proofs of the authenticity of my communication with Galia is that as a *baalas teshuva* at the beginning of my journey, I could not have had any previous knowledge of the things that Galia wrote out for me on the alphabet board.

In fact, Galia did not state anything new for a person already in the world of Torah and *mitzvos*. But for myself, a person very far from the world of Torah and *mitzvos* (and for those like me), the communication process and Galia's messages were total eye-openers! For me, they were like the discovery of America. To my complete surprise, the rabbi who checked the messages of Galia confirmed that the messages were sourced in the Talmud, *Mishna*, *Zohar*, *Chazal* and other classic Jewish sources — things which I do not have the faintest idea or understanding of.

In one particular session, Galia wrote out a message telling me to go to a certain rabbi. She wrote out the name of the rabbi and his address.

As a *baalas teshuva* taking her first steps, I hadn't been able to decide which rabbi to take as my counselor. Galia chose a great rabbi who is a well known *tzadik,* and one of the major halachic authorities of our time. The rabbi encouraged me to give talks to women. Of course, he explained, there is no prohibition on communicating by means of FC. The Torah states, "Do not seek out the dead," meaning it is forbidden to communicate with dead spirits. Seances or any other form of communication with the dead are a serious offense and involve enormous *tum'ah*. I communicate with the living, with the soul of a living person, and therefore there is no prohibition.

The rabbis forbid consulting people with mental incompetence and autism as though they are our *Urim v'Tumim*. It is important to stress that if a person has a question, he should consult a rabbi and obtain the Torah's answer to his question. Galia wrote, "*Rabbanim* are the messengers of Hashem. And those who refer personal questions to people with autism are likely to compromise the requirement to apply free choice in their lives and possibly ruin their *tikun* in this world too."

Great and famous rabbis, yeshiva principals, great scholars and halachic authorities who have examined all of Galia's messages confirm that all of Galia's messages are remarkably similar to what is found in traditional source works. They have even recommended to their students to read them, obviously warning them at the same time to apply all the caution necessary in using Facilitated Communication.

✤ *Understanding FC From The Torah*

The rabbis explain the workings of Facilitated Communication from a Torah standpoint. My understanding of their teachings is as follows:

The Talmud in *Maseches Nida* (30:2) states of the embryo in the womb of its mother that: "A light shines over its head and it observes and sees from one end of the world to the other."

How can an embryo, whose eyes are closed and is inside the womb of its mother, see everything that takes place from one end of the world to the other? The Talmud explains "A light shines over its head" — as referring to the *neshama*, the soul, whose powers of vision are not limited. The soul is that which sees from one end of the world to the other, as well as all of the secrets of the higher worlds.

Rabbi Eliyahu Dessler *zt"l* explained: "These perceptions certainly do not come to the embryo through the brain. Rather, they are perceptions of the inner being which flow onto his spirit without the limitations of time and place." *Michtav MiEliyahu* (volume IV, pg. 163)

The powers of the sight of the soul are not limited to the eyes. We are but transparent beings. The following incident will illustrate this. A certain brain-damaged child, who used FC to communicate, turned up in school one day noisy and excited. He made sounds and behaved wildly. The teacher gave him a spelling board and asked him to write why he was so rowdy that day. The child wrote, "I'm so happy that you are expecting twins!" The surprised teacher was unaware that she was pregnant. Pregnancy tests proved positive, and a subsequent ultra-sound scan showed that she was indeed carrying twins.

The Talmud also says in *Maseches Nida* (ibid), "They teach the infant the whole Torah." How can an infant in the womb acquire knowledge of the whole Torah, which is wider than the seas, during just nine months of pregnancy, while we study Torah all our lives and still don't manage to learn everything? The answer is, again, that the statement refers to the soul. The soul is a *"chelek elokah mima'al,"* a part and parcel of the *Shechina*. It is not limited by the speed or the quantity of material to be absorbed.

The Talmud in *Maseches Baba Basra* (12:2) states, "From the day the *Beis Hamikdash* was destroyed ... prophecy was given to imbeciles and infants."

Harav Dessler in *Michtav MiEliyahu*, (ibid) explains, *"Prophesy was given to imbeciles —* because their screen [i.e., filter] is not so strong."

As we have seen, the soul knows and perceives everything, with no limitations. It is only in our world of darkness, *olam hazeh*, wherein the soul is housed in the human body, that its powers are intentionally limited by G-d in order to allow us to function normally. During this period, a human being perceives his surroundings by means of his flesh-and-blood brain, which is essentially limited and acts as a filter for the soul. The brain of a mentally disabled person, however, is damaged. This means that the screen covering the soul is incomplete. There is no concealment or material covering. When the brain is damaged, the soul is freed, and has no limitations and sees everything. This also allows **us** a glimpse into the world of the soul. The brain is that which limits and conceals the soul.

The Zohar, *parshas Shemos*, 6:2, states: "Rebbe Chiyya said, 'Thirty days prior to a country receiving power and strength or before a country goes through crisis and destruction, they announce the matter throughout the whole world. Sometimes the matter is passed on to the mouth of infants and sometimes to those imbecilic people who have no minds. Sometimes the matter is passed on to the mouth of birds. They announce the news in the world and there is no one who will see [hear] and understand the announcement. When the nation is composed of men of *zechus* and *tzadikim*, the affair is passed onto the leaders, the *tzadikim* of the world, in order that they inform the people of the decree so that they will return to G-d. But when the nation is not composed of men of *zechus*, the procedure adopted, as we said, is that the affair is placed in the mouths of infants or imbeciles or birds. The people are not aware of the matter so they are not prompted to do *teshuva* and prevent the implementation of the decree."

Today, *baruch Hashem*, we are aware of the fact that "imbeciles" know the truth. They pass it on to us to open our eyes and prompt us to do *teshuva*. The person who hears and contemplates their message is in a fortunate position. Hashem has had mercy on us and the truth is now starting to be revealed in this world of falsity.

Chapter Two: The Discovery of Facilitated Communication

"גל עיני"

Open my eyes so I can see the wonders of your Torah.

Tehillim 119:18

Chapter Two

❧ Carol Lee Berger's Discovery of FC in the U.S.

ichard was a seven-year-old autistic child who suffered from severe brain damage. He did not speak, and wandered around the classroom aimlessly while holding his ears and making unusual noises.

One day, Carol Lee Berger, a communications disorders specialist, decided that she would show Richard her personal computer. She sat Richard in front of the PC. Fearing that the child would throw the monitor or the printer to the floor, she placed a chair behind the child and sat behind him in order to be able to control his hand movements and show him the keyboard. She held his hand and together they typed out his name. She moved his hand over all the letters.

A few days later, Carol sat down with Richard again and said to him, "Let's type your name." Before Carol could move Richard's hand, she felt that he was moving his hand by himself to the letters of his name. She thought she was imagining things. Richard proceeded to type out his whole name by himself.

Carol showed him on the computer a picture of a dog and told him, "Touch the dog." Instead of touching the picture, Richard moved his hand to the word dog that was written out at the bottom of the screen (as one of a selection of three words) and touched it. Carol showed him a picture of a pumpkin, and said to him, "Touch the pumpkin." Richard touched the word pumpkin, which was one of a choice of three words at the bottom of the screen. Carol showed him a picture of a gate and Richard again touched the word instead of the picture. He succeeded in identifying dozens of words, although he was never taught to read.

Carol tried this with her other brain-damaged and autistic pupils and got 100% results with all the pupils! Since then, Carol Lee Berger has succeeded in communicating tens of thousands of times with children suffering from mental deficiency.

✢✍ *Carol Lee And Her Communication With Myrna Miller*

One adult with whom Carol Lee Berger worked was Myrna Miller, aged 34. She was an autistic woman living in Springfield, Oregon, who communicated with her mother through FC. Her mother, Phyllis, founded the Autism Society of Oregon. She tells of how she discovered the fact that her daughter had completely normal intelligence: "She was trying to verbally tell me something one day, trying to speak. She grabbed hold of a pencil and with my support began to write what she wanted."

For over twenty-nine months, Myrna went to the local public school every day for forty-five minutes. Eventually the school asked her parents to remove her. Today she is capable of solving complicated algebra problems and writing stories rich in language and feeling, using hand support to write with a pencil or type on a computer keyboard. Her parents purchased course material for home study when her term in school came to a quick and sudden end. "We started with the kindergarten level and worked our way up to seventh grade," Phyllis reported. Myrna now reads her mother's engineering books and does academic courses broadcasted daily on educational television.

In her book, Facilitated Communication Guide, Carol Lee Berger has provided numerous examples of how others who are defined as having average, severe, or highly severe mental retardation, or as having autism, cerebral palsy or Down's syndrome, are able to communicate at various levels using FC — even to the extent of using it without the assistance of a facilitator. Commenting on the evolution of FC, Ms. Berger writes,"The development of Facilitated Communication (FC) did not happen in one isolated place in the world, but was independently discovered in Sweden, the United States, Canada, and Australia by individuals who were all driven to find ways to help autistic people communicate."

❧ The Pioneering Work of Rosemary Crossley

In the 1970's in Australia, Rosemary Crossley, a pioneer in the field of FC, worked in an institution for the physically handicapped. She would make use of hand or forearm support in order to help patients with cerebral palsy gain more control over their movements, to slow them down and give them a more reasonable possibility of achieving precise movement direction. In 1986, Rosemary Crossley had her first FC communication with a mentally hadicapped person, Jonothan Solaris. Jonothan was a seven year old boy who was classified as autistic. Handsome, incapable of speaking, and not toilet-trained, Jonothan would snatch items he wanted, would not make eye contact, and gazed vacantly. He would walk on the balls of his feet in a manner akin to prancing. In addition, Jonothan had a history of temper tantrums and shouting, of clawing himself and of running away from people.

Rosemary Crossley suggested to Jonothan's mother that she leave they boy with her one afternoon. She succeeded in calming him down by attracting his attention to a small electric Canon computer. As she held his wrist, Jonathan pressed on the keys she touched. She typed out "Jonathan" and then "Mom," and then asked him to type out "Dad." Without wrist support, he went straight for the letter D, and then for the letter A. Then with wrist support but without being directed, he completed the word Dad. Then Rosemary typed out the word JONATHAN. He corrected her and typed out JONOTHAN. Later on, Rosemary checked up on the spelling of his name and it turned out that Jonothan was correct.

Ms. Crossley guided him through the entire alphabet on the keyboard. She then asked him what letter the word "good" started with. He pressed G. She asked how many fingers she had on one hand. He pressed 5. She asked how many on two hands; he pressed 10. "If you took 5 from 10, how many would you have left?" she then asked. He typed 5. She continued, "5 plus 3?" He answered 8. They continued in this manner, with Jonothan giving answers to general questions and to various math exercises.

Ms. Crossley, together with another colleague, founded the Center for Facilitated Communication in Australia, called DEAL (Dignity through Education and Language), for those who are unable to speak, or have speech impairment. In addition to lecturing throughout the world, she has written many articles and books, and has produced videos containing documented proof of the validity of the FC method.

❧ *Professor Biklen's Research On Facilitated Communication*

Professor Douglas Biklen of the University of Syracuse, New York, who has also done much important work in documenting the FC field, devoted himself to a thorough examination of the application of FC by institutions and individuals in the States and in Australia. He coordinated all of his findings and knowledge on the matter. On the basis of this, as well as on the basis of his own research, he set up the Facilitated Communication Institute at the University of Syracuse in New York State.

In an article he wrote entitled Communication Unbound: Autism and Praxis (Harvard Educational Review, no. 3, 1990), Biklen describes how he received a letter from Australia in July 1987 (before he had accomplished his major works), and was very surprised to read of the success of Rosemary Crossley with Facilitated Communication. At that time it was a brand new method that reportedly enabled people with autism to communicate on a sophisticated level. The letter described how the method also worked with students who were previously classified as having a low level of functioning and a lack of basic intellectual ability.

"I didn't know what to make of this," Professor Biklen wrote. He could not accept the fact that people with autism, who were classically defined as having serious intellectual deficiency, could turn out to be people with a regular, or even close to regular, standard of literacy. Twice in 1989, Professor Biklen traveled to DEAL in Melbourne. He wrote, "On my first visit to Melbourne, Australia, by chance, the same afternoon that I interviewed Mrs. Crossley, Jonothan came to the DEAL communication center. Rosemary told him that we were speaking of the first time he printed on the Canon. She asked him if he remembered what his first word was. (Three years had elapsed.) She handed him the small electric computer. Without support Jonothan typed "Dad" and then immediately added, "Jonothan not Jonathan."

Biklen further related that Rosemary Crossley got a group of four students together and gave them the assignment of trying to find out as much about him [Biklen] as possible. Rather than investigating the dry facts about him, the students preferred to inquire about his views, beliefs and philosophy of life. They went into a deep debate about values and ideologies. They showed humor and responded critically to remarks that people had made. In his view, there was no sign of any intellectual deficiency. Often, it was the students who took the initiative in sharing their feelings with their facilitators. To Professor Biklen's trained eye, there did not appear to be any issues of learning ability or sensitivity at all, but rather a communication deficiency in conveying thoughts and feelings to the external environment.

❧ The Session With Louis

Professor Biklen also described in his article how he witnessed the very first communication session between Rosemary and a non-speaking autistic resident named Louis Armbruster. This took place at an adult training center for disabled people who are capable of working under supervision.

"Crossley introduced herself and me to Louis. She apologized to him in advance: 'Louis, I ask people a lot of really silly questions.' She then asked him to press on various pictures shown on a computer screen. To assist him, she put her hand on top of his right forearm. Louis responded to the instructions of the computer, for example, 'Press the red car, the small square, and the large triangle.' Louis responded correctly. The next task was to point at a particular requested word from a number of words, for example, point to the word clock. Once again, Louis correctly identified all the words. After that he was asked to find words inside sentences. He found them all without error. Finally, Rosemary asked Louis to point at certain letters, and again he was correct. Then Rosemary decided to show Louis a Canon Communicator. First she went over all the letters and numbers that were on it together with him. Then she turned to him and said, 'Can you type your name?' At this point, her hand was completely spead over his hand, without actually being in contact with it. Touching the keyboard he proceeded to type his first name: Louis. He also typed out his surname. Rosemary then asked him if he had something to say. He wrote out, 'I am not retarded.' Rosemary replied, 'I didn't think you were — keep going.' Louis went on to spell out, 'My mother thinks that I am stupid because I can't use my voice properly.' A tear rolled down his left cheek as he typed. Rosemary said to him, 'Anyone who starts off typing, *I'm not retarded,* isn't retarded.' "

Professor Biklen concluded in his article that the problem experienced by people with autism and mental incompetence was not a problem in their ability to comprehend, but rather a difficulty in their ability to communicate what they know and feel. In other words, Biklen wrote, what these individuals have is a neurologically based problem of expression. People who suffer from developmental deficiency, especially those suffering from autism, have difficulties in mustering words. It can be argued that they suffer from developmental dyspraxia, which creates a situation in which producing communication is difficult because of their inability to control their motoric movements.

❧ Discovery of The FC Technique By Nobel Prize Winner Dr. Schawlow and His Wife Aurelia

In 1983, Dr. Schawlow, a Nobel Prize winner in physics and one of the developers of the laser, publicized his discovery of FC, which he used to communicate with his autistic son Artie. Born in 1956, Artie never responded to his parents' communications, and at the age of five was classified as autistic. It was at this point that his parents then began an endless search for help in treating their son. Dr. Schawlow said, "Physicians told us to place Artie in an institution and forget about him."

The Discovery of Facilitated Communication 49

It was Dr. Schawlow's prestige that enabled them to seek help for Artie in whichever part of the world they visited. But at the age of twenty-five, Artie still did not speak, and his only means of communicating was via facial expressions and hand gestures. However, the Schawlows were not prepared to give up their search for a means of communication with their beloved son. In 1981, when they were in Stockholm attending the Nobel Prize award ceremony, they met Dr. Karin Stensland Junker, a psychologist and the mother of an autistic child. Dr. Junker told the couple about a twenty-four year old man who had visited her in her practice. He seemed to have a typical case of autism except for the fact that he used a small writing device in order to communicate. The couple regarded this as a dramatic piece of information. When they returned to the States, they bought Artie a Canon Communicator, the same device that the young man had used. Unlike this young man, however, Artie typed out only a few letters over and over again — such as XXZZZ — without typing any words. The device was then set aside for almost two years.

Mrs. Aurelia Schawlow tried to teach Artie to read. "We found Artie could pick out any word on a page of a book. Even more surprising, he could pick out words from a magazine page, even one as difficult as the *New Yorker.*" The couple did not then understand that Artie was capable of much more than identifying words on a page.

Eventually, Artie was kept in the district hospital. The staff was unwilling to keep a computer in the ward permanently. So the couple would bring in a small battery-operated computer at every opportunity. These computers made use of a small program in Basic, which was programmed to show a word on a screen with each letter underlined. Artie had to match the next letter of the word displayed on the screen. When the word was completed, a printer that was attached to the computer printed it out.

"The first time we tried it, he [Artie] did it eagerly for more than an hour until the tape ran out and then he stuffed the printer tapes into his pocket," recalls Dr. Schawlow.

One day in the hospital, Artie started to wave his arms wildly and point in a certain direction. Instead of trying to guess what he was trying to say, the Schawlows took out the Canon, which had not been used now for two years. "We didn't really expect it to work, but Aurelia took his hand and he typed 'SHOES' and indeed, there was a shoe store across the street. We took him there and bought shoes for him."

Later he printed what he wanted to eat and where he wanted to go. His last request that day demonstrated his feelings. When his parents were ready to leave, Artie typed, "Stay your time with me. I want to go home." Artie went home the same day and never returned to that hospital again. From that point onward the Schawlows kept their son at home, together with a group of people like him.

The Schawlows tried to get Artie to use the computer without any assistance. "Sometimes he would if he was especially eager," said Aurelia Schawlow. But most of the time, he wanted hand support to reassure and assist him.

A number of years after this, by which time they were using the form of FC that they had developed, Artie told them that, "I learned to read when I was ten."

This statement itself is worthy of thorough investigation. How many of us can say when exactly we learned to read? Could it be possible that he learned to read without years of training and exercises? Others who suffer from autism, when communicating for the first time, also report on having already having gained reading and arithmetic skills at an earlier point in time.

In 1985, Dr. Schawlow was featured in a European film about Nobel Prize winners. When the camera crew came to the States, he invited them home to see his son. None of the film crew had ever seen anyone classified as autistic before. Artie took out his Canon Communicator and put it on the table. Almost without looking at the keys, he took his mother's hand and began to type out messages. Aurelia looked at the camera and said, "Don't ask me how he does it, but he does it without looking. Maybe he's got peripheral vision or something." It has been demonstrated that people with autism and retardation often do not have to look directly at the keyboard, or that they seem to memorize it almost instantaneously.

The Schawlows noted, "We are convinced that the main reason that many adults with autism appear to be unable to learn is because so few people try to reach them and to teach them."

In 1983 and 1985, Artie's parents published articles in newspapers about their success in using the technique of physical help through supporting the hand of their son, Artie. In 1985, they delivered a paper on the subject in a world conference on autism in Los Angeles.

Dr. Schawlow emotionally described the first time Artie communicated with them as being the happiest moment of his life. "Communication with Artie was more important to me than the moment when I won the Nobel Prize."

The FC communication method has also been featured in a number of prominent television programs on local U.S. networks, as well as other national and international networks. Some of these programs include: CBS News' *The Evening Edition* with Dan Rather, July 21,1993; *How Do They Do It?* on CBS, September 17,1993; *Frontline* on October 19,1983; and *60 Minutes,* in February 1994. Most recently there has ben a *60 Minutes II* segment on January 15, 2003, demonstrating a similar method of communication requiring no hand support at all. The *New York Times,* the *Washington Post,* the *Post Standard* and the *Herald Journal* have also published articles on the topic of FC.

Today Facilitated Communication is recognized and in use in most of the western world. In the U.S. alone, thirty-eight states include it in their education program, and at the University of Syracuse there are seven students who are researching their doctorates in FC.

Despite the fact that researchers are still debating the authenticity of FC, its success in helping people is a fact that is very hard to ignore or refute. Today FC institutes are continually being opened in most of the countries in the western world.

❧ The Beginnings Of FC In Israel

FC was introduced in Israel in April 1992 by two facilitators who had learned the method in the United States. Mrs. Chani Chukat, at Bar Ilan University, wrote a pioneering M.A. thesis in the summer of 1998, entitled, "Parents' Attitudes Toward Their Severely Retarded Children After the Children's Exposure to An Alternative Communication Channel." Mrs. Chukat's thesis, in which she tracked the progress of children with serious mental incompetence, found that after exposure to FC, assessors considered most of the children as being of sound intelligence. More importantly, the parents of such children treated them completely differently than parents of disabled children who did not experience the benefits of FC. Regarding the religious community's acceptance of FC, Professor Avraham Steinberg wrote in an article entitled, "Facilitated Communication with Autistic and Retarded Children" (published by Assia, the foundation for medical research under the auspices of Sha'arei Tzedek Hospital in Jerusalem): "The FC technique was promoted by the kabalist, Rabbi Weintraub of Bnei Brak, and subsequently by Rabbi Yehuda Srevnik of Jerusalem."

Many Israeli institutions employ the technique in classes for children who use it to communicate their day to day requirements. The child denotes his desires, feelings, and the events of his daily life linked to food, sleep, pains, etc. There is also a yeshiva in Israel where the students study the Talmud using FC!

Presently in Israel, the FC technique can be learned only via trained professionals such as communication therapists, special education teachers or experienced facilitators. As of yet, there is still no official FC training institution. Parents desperate to learn how to communicate with their children must take their own initiative to establish contact with the very few facilitators that are present in the country today in order to learn the technique.

❧ Facilitated Communication and Prevailing Attitudes

Beyond looking at the techniques and the phenomenon of FC itself, we must also take a look at the prevailing attitudes of the special education community and the population served by it.

We may be witnessing a phenomenon — the uncovering of people wrongly labeled as retarded. Those who for years could not convey feelings, emotions, wants, desires and needs in their daily life now have access to communication, and through it can reveal their inherent intelligence.

We must ask whether attitudes have prevented or curtailed an earlier revelation of the cognitive abilities of people labeled as "mentally retarded". Do prevailing views about disabilities warrant attacks on the method of Facilitated Communication? Is the system so indoctrinated in old values that it seeks to devalue any possible solution or intervention that is scientifically unproven? Outdated models and assumptions that no longer serve the population need to be shed, while the ever-increasing evidence on the success of role of FC needs to be implemented.

Chapter Three:
Proofs of the Authenticity of Facilitated Communication and of Galia's Messages

---

**There is one thing stronger than
all the armies in the world,
and that is an idea
whose time has come.**

Victor Hugo

Chapter Three

here is a great deal of controversy over the issue of Facilitated Communication. Any historic breakthrough of great proportions, especially one such as this, aspects of which are virtually unexplainable by science, tends to immediately divide the research community into those that are "for" and those that are "against". Opponents of FC maintain that the facilitator influences the response of the FC user, whether by overtly pushing the hand, or by subconsciously expecting a certain answer and then spelling it out. Some even feel that there is some sort of mental telepathy taking place between the facilitator and the user (as if that would be a "scientific" explanation!). Proponents of the method point to several incontrovertible proofs, some of which are mentioned here, that repeat themselves in hundreds of cases. Professor Biklen himself admits that it is not always possible to validate FC by observation, since in most cases the FC user requires support in order to achieve motoric accuracy. This fact, in and of itself, creates the difficulty of proving the source of the communication through classic research laboratory testing.

Despite the dilemmas involved in scientifically confirming the validity of Facilitated Communication, the following proofs show the authenticity of the FC method from a logical standpoint, and I believe that they speak for themselves.

✺ Proof #1 –
Communicating Without a Facilitator

One of the decisive proofs of the authenticity of FC is the fact that there are many people with autism and other mental problems who eventually overcome the need for hand support to use the technique. They are then able to communicate independently and type their thoughts and wishes by themselves, unaided by a facilitator.

Some people make do with just light, partial support, such as touching them on the sleeve, the shoulder, or the head. I possess certified films from the U.S., Australia, and other countries that show people communicating by themselves without the help of a facilitator at all. (These films have been shown numerous times on Israeli TV on scientific and educational channels.) I also have a documentary video from the University of Syracuse which was recorded at a conference in front of an audience of thousands, of a brain-damaged person communicating independently, without any support at all. In addition, one newsclip shows a young girl, defined as having autism, communicating with light support. The facilitator touches her sleeve or shirt and she points to the letters on the board and writes. Additional examples of this method are demonstrated on videos produced by Rosemary Crossley, who is shown facilitating by lightly touching the shoulders of people who are attempting to communicate through FC.

The fact that sometimes only minimal assistance, or none at all, is administered by a facilitator during an FC session, lends much authenticity to the method of Facilitated Communication.

❧ *Proof #2 – Facilitator Unaware of Information*

The content of the printed message itself sometimes proves that it comes from the user and not from the facilitator. According to Professor Biklen: "Sometimes brain-damaged users produce messages whose content the facilitator has no prior knowledge of."

For example (one of many):

a) Jennifer wrote a story about her dog called Dorsi. Her instructor commented: "But you haven't got a dog." When Jennifer's mother came later, it emerged that the family once had a dog named Dorsi.

b) When the facilitator asked Bryan from Australia if he was expecting both of his parents to come to visit afterwards or just one of them, he typed "Both of them." Indeed, later his two parents came to take him.

As a result of her work in the field of FC, Rosemary Crossley became a defendant in a court case in Australia that questioned the legitimacy of FC and its practices. Its challengers alleged that it was in fact the facilitator who was selecting the letters that were typed and not the child. They claimed that children with mental incompetence were incapable of typing a meaningful sentence, and therefore FC might involve deception. To assess this the court conducted various tests. One such test was as follows: Children who were FC users were presented with items in the absence of the facilitator. The facilitator had no knowledge of this.

These items were then placed in a closed box. Upon the facilitator's return to the courtroom, the children were asked to identify the contents of the box with the assistance of the facilitator. The children did this accurately. The High Court of Victoria, Australia, ruled in favor of Rosemary Crossley, that the children alone were the authors of what they wrote, thereby confirming the authenticity of the FC method.

Similarly, a group of psychologists, speech experts and educators in Australia tested the authenticity of FC by distributing gifts to some mentally disabled students without facilitators knowing what the gifts were. The students were then asked to identify the gifts through these facilitators. Nearly all of them succeeded in doing so.

❧ *Proof #3 – Facial Expressions and Reactions Indicate Authorship*

Facial expressions, sounds, laughter or other signs are testimony to the fact that the person communicating knows what he or she is saying. For example, Louis, in the communication session with Rosemary Crossley mentioned earlier, wrote, "I am not retarded. My mother thinks I am stupid." A tear emerged from his left eye as he typed. Countless similar forthright remarks testifying to the sophisticated level of understanding on the part of disabled individuals are on record in Israel as well as in the U.S. and Australia. These testify to the fact that the communications are coming directly from the disabled person and not from the facilitator.

❧ *Proof #4 – Individual Styles*

The character and style of FC communication varies from user to user, even if the same facilitator has been employed. Conversely, one user may maintain his individual style although communicating through different facilitators. One even sees patterns of mistakes unique to each user.

On this subject, Professor Biklen lists the following observations in support of the argument that the source of the spelled-out messages is the FC user, not the facilitator:

- Each brain-damaged user tends to make spelling errors peculiar to him, regardless of which facilitator is working with him.
- The aspects of the user's writing style are particular to him.
- The style and pace of the refined motoric movements relative to the alphabet board or keyboard are consistent even if facilitators change.
- Some brain-damaged users compose unusual sentences and phrases, which one cannot reasonably presume were authored by the facilitator.
- The individual personality of the brain-damaged person comes through in the style and composition of the messages.

✢ᘗ *Proof #5 – FC User Reveals Hidden Information*

There are many instances in which the FC user supplied information which was unknown, not only to the facilitator, but to anyone else in the room, and at times even to the child's parents. Sometimes this information was only verified later on.

On January 1, 2000, the newspaper Kol Bo, which is circulated in Haifa and the north of Israel, published an article on communication with Galia. It seems that in preparing the article, the journalist contacted the headmistress of a school for autistic children in Haifa to obtain her reaction to FC. The principal, Mrs. Shula Kalish, evidently responded that she would contact one of the mothers whom she knew had experimented with FC, sure that this mother would give a negative report.

Instead the child's mother answered as follows: "Five years ago, I contacted a facilitator in Zichron Yaakov and asked her if she would teach me FC. My daughter was then 11. After three meetings without much success, the facilitator told me she would not go on. I brought my sister and asked if she would teach her. With her it worked.

Question: What messages did your daughter pass on?

Mother: She knew that she is named for my husband's great-great grandmother, something that my sister did not know. There were messages about it being hard for her and her role in the world. She continually wanted to talk about her father and that surprised us, because in fact she had no special link with him.

There is a lot of telepathy involved. You can feel it in her answers. For example, once a girl was here from national service [i.e. to help look after the daughter] and through my sister, she asked my young daughter many questions. Some of the questions dealt with the character of her friend, and one question was to predict the mark she would get on an exam she was soon to take. My daughter passed on a precise picture of the characteristics of the girl's friend, and also wrote down the mark she would get. After a few days, the girl phoned up excited and said that that was the mark she got.

Another time, we were in my sister's house and we asked my daughter what my mother is doing now. My daughter answered, "Fixing the soup." We rang up my mother's home and found out that at that moment she was putting spices in the soup.

Question: Did it have any influence on you?

Mother: My husband and I did not go through any change. My brother, however, did teshuva as a result of this.

✺ Proof #6 – Courts Admit FC Evidence

An article appeared in the press some time ago, and also on an FC website, entitled "Some Courts Are Now Accepting Testimony Given Through Facilitated Communication." Details were given of two court cases, one in Wichita, Kansas, and the other one involving the Family Court of Orange County and the Supreme Court of New York State, in which FC testimony was deemed an admissible form of evidence.

In the Wichita case, which took place in March of 1993, FC evidence was accepted in a case involving the abuse of a brain-damaged boy. The jury found the accused guilty. I have a short clip of this trial that was shown in the United States and throughout the world on cable television.

In the case that came before the Family Court of Orange County in January of 1993, the prosecutor wanted to use FC testimony to establish that the defendant had abused Miss Luz P. He also suggested to the court a simple method for proving the reliability of Luz P.'s evidence. The defense objected, claiming that even if the prosecutor could prove his claim, the science of FC had not come into widespread acceptance and that therefore legal precedent would not allow new evidence based on such sciences. The Supreme Court of New York overruled this on March 29, 1993, and allowed the prosecutor to demonstrate his case. In general, courts are now willing to consider FC as evidence.

✣ Proof #7 – User's Reaction to FC

Perhaps the most obvious and compelling proof that the communication comes from the user and not the facilitator are the thousands of users worldwide who use FC to communicate their daily needs and who respond to the communication accordingly.

For example (one of many):

a) Chaim, an autistic boy, was sitting by the table and crying. When the facilitator asked him what was wrong, he responded that he did not want to have a peanut butter sandwich for lunch, that he did not like peanut butter. When his mother gave him an egg instead, he calmed down and began to eat happily.

b) Rina, a mentally disabled girl in a wheelchair, started shrieking for no apparent reason. Upon questioning, she insisted that she wanted to go to the park with her younger siblings, who were getting ready to go. The children agreed to take her, and she stopped shouting.

Instances like these are the most common usages of FC, and are also the most obvious proof. How could the facilitator have known which answer to give that would calm down the child? Common sense dictates that the child, not the facilitator, composed the reply.

✣ Proofs of the Authenticity of the Communications With Galia

Proof #1 — The First Communication with Galia

My very first encounter with Facilitated Communication provided me with powerful proof of its authenticity.

As you will recall, prior to my first session with Galia, I prepared a list of questions to ask her. I included the statement "Galia, I love you" at the top to remind me to convey this most important point.

As detailed in Part I, Galia began her "speaking career" with "Ima, I love you" and proceeded to answer every single question on my list before I even had a chance to ask her one of them. She also supplied the names of my grandparents. The facilitator, who was a total stranger to me, obviously did not have access to my notes, nor to the names of my grandparents, some of whom had died before I was born.

Proof #2 — Messages Which I Had No Means Of Knowing Myself

Another one of the most decisive proofs of the authenticity of the communication with Galia, which was mentioned earlier, was that she wrote messages to me which appear in the *Zohar, Kabala, Gemara, Mishna,* and other sources. These were things that I had no means of knowing myself, certainly not in the months after I became religious.

Within a few months of my first FC session, I learned to communicate with Galia myself. Galia wrote me amazing messages of which I had no understanding, messages on the subjects of *Mashiach*, redemption, angels, the *gilgul* of souls, old age, dreams, the *shefa* descending from the holy of holies in Heaven, the composition of the incenses burnt in the Temple, *Song of Songs*, suffering, and more.

As I already recounted, Galia sent me to a great rabbi, who looked over the messages and validated every one of them, finding sources in all the classic texts. All of this material, which was totally foreign to me, was known to Galia's soul. Galia knows the whole Torah. The *Mishna*, the *Zohar*, everything. Communication with Galia is with her soul and not with her mind. Galia only has the mental capacity of a baby.

❧ Examples Which Authenticate My Words

First Example

In one of the sessions, Galia wrote me an amazing message about Jerusalem.

> Galia: Ima, Jerusalem is the holy city and every grain in that town is full of holiness and wrapped in it. It is considered a very big *zechus* for anyone who can live in holy Jerusalem. He will be surrounded by *kedusha ila'is* [high holiness]. Of all countries, the land of Israel is the holiest of all of them.
>
> And of all the cities in the land of Israel, Jerusalem is the holiest of them.
>
> And of all the sites in Jerusalem, the Temple Mount is the holiest of all of them. And the site of the Holy Of Holies is the holiest place in the world. It is the entrance gate for the divine *shefa* which *HaKadosh Baruch Hu* in His great mercy and love for His precious Jewish people showers down on us from Heaven.

Ima, now Jerusalem is a destroyed city and *HaKadosh Baruch Hu* is pained over its destruction, and the destruction of His beloved Jewish people. Also the Jerusalem in Heaven is sad and is waiting for the big lights to be lit up in it, soon, *be-ezras Hashem Yisbarach*.

All of the *mitzvos* of the Jewish people light shining and radiant lights in it. When the Jewish nation returns to our Father in Heaven, the Jerusalem in Heaven fills with happiness and joy.

I thought, in my ignorance, that Galia was revealing some Heavenly secrets. I was even a little afraid. It turned out that Galia was conveying a message contained in the *Zohar (parshas Teruma)*: "The Holy Land is the center of the world and the middle of the Holy Land is Jerusalem and the middle of Jerusalem is the House of the Holy of Holies, and all the good and all the sustenance of the whole world, comes down there from above, and there is nowhere in the world which does not receive its sustenance from there.

"The dominion of the secret of faith is within the central point of the entire Holy Land in the House of the Holy of Holies. Even though it does not exist at present, its *zechus* feeds and supplies the entire world. Food and sustenance go from there to everyone. Even though the Jewish people are outside the Holy Land, food and sustenance exist in the world through the power and *zechus* of the land."

Midrash Tanchuma (Introduction, *Kedoshim*) states: "The Holy Land is the navel of the world since it occupies the middle. And Jerusalem is in the middle of Israel. And the *Beis Hamikdash* is in the middle of Jerusalem. And the Inner Temple is in the middle of the *Beis Hamikdash*. And the Ark is in the middle of the Inner Temple. And the Source Stone [*even hashesiya*] from which the world flows, is in front of the Inner Temple."

It is extraordinary how close Galia's message on Jerusalem is to our original holy sources. Is it possible that I could have written down concepts from the *Zohar*, and the *Midrash* which I had never before seen or heard?! Is it possible that I could record things that I didn't know?!

Second Example

In one session, Galia conveyed an extraordinary message, which left me speechless.

Galia explained to me that: "Fulfilling *mitzvos* in this world custom-tailors splendorous clothing for a person, of beauty impossible to fathom. Everyone is dressed in accordance with his deeds in this world.

"In the next world, there is no such thing as being without a body. Each world has the body appropriate to that world and its purpose. In the next world, which is a spiritual world, there are spiritual clothes. And the clothes a person wears depends entirely on his actions and to what extent he has rectified himself in this world.

"So it's extremely important to fulfill the *mitzvos* and do *maasim tovim*. Each *mitzva* builds our glorious spiritual clothing and decorates them with countless adornments.

"Those who do not do *mitzvos* here are in a pathetic plight in the next world — because what have they to wear? They are naked! And they do not have another chance of getting clothes. That possibility exists only in this world.

"They are dependent upon the favors of others, for their only chance is that someone will do a good deed for them in this world. There is no guarantee that somebody will.

"The most bitter fate that a person can have is to arrive in the next world without *mitzvos*. He is in a really pitiful state. It's shameful for his soul because it has no clothes.

"In this world when a man is poor and destitute, he has no clothing. He freezes in the rain and in winter. In the summer, he goes around ashamed as well. Everyone sees that he does not have any clothing.

"In the next world, everything is clear: if he has no clothes, then we all know that he has no *mitzvos*.

"So, Ima, *mitzvos* create the most beautiful clothing. You don't have such beautiful clothes in this world. You can't even imagine how beautiful they are." After hearing this from Galia, I was informed that the *Zohar* (*parshas Teruma*) states the same thing almost word for word:

When a spirit leaves there (Heaven) for this world, the body and the clothes of the Garden of Eden are removed from him and he is dressed in the body and clothes of this world. He makes his abode in this world, in this clothing and in this body, which is the product of a putrid drop.

And when the time comes for him to leave this world, he does not go until the Angel of Death removes this clothing and body. Since the Angel of Death has removed the body from the spirit, the spirit goes and dresses itself in the other body, that of the Garden of Eden which was removed from it when it came into this world.

The spirit can have no happiness there without that body. And it is happy to be rid of the body of this world and to be dressed in the other, perfect clothing of the Garden of Eden, which is like that world. With that body, he sits and walks and searches to find the higher secrets — secrets that he cannot know and see while he is in this world in this body.

And when the soul dresses in the clothing of that world, how many delights and how many joys he has there!

HaKadosh Baruch Hu performs a kindness to mandkind by not divesting man of his clothing in this world until He prepares for him finer and more wonderful clothes than these, in *Gan Eden*. But the wicked of this world who do not fully repent to their Master before dying come naked to this world and return there naked. And the soul goes around feeling shame before the other souls because it has no clothing at all.

Similarly, *Yalkut Meam Loez, Bereshis,* part I states:

In the second chamber of Heaven, there are many types of clothes that good Jews are invited to wear before appearing before *HaKadosh Baruch Hu.* For every *mitzva* which a man does in this world, with the right intention, for the sake of Heaven, the appointees for this activity in that chamber prepare a pleasant outfit for him. If the soul is very pure, it leaves the Dinur River quickly and they dress him in that outfit and bring him to Heaven in the charge of the angel Michael.

If it is a soul bare of *mitzvos* and polluted from sin, they push him to the other side of the chamber and there hordes of angels of punishment beat him until they drag him away to *Gehinom.*

There is also the well-known story of the glorious outfit that the "Maggid" angel revealed to *Rabeinu Maran,* the Beis Yosef, of blessed memory. The angel wore this in his constant appearances before the Beis Yosef to exhibit the outfit the Beis Yosef would wear in the next world.

Proof #3 — Different Children Using Different Facilitators Pass On Identical Messages

It is extraordinary to discover that different mentally disabled children in different parts of the world, who communicate through different facilitators, and have no link to each other at all, write out the same messages on the same spiritual subjects, and with almost identical language! This demonstrates the authenticity of FC and the authenticity of the communication with Galia.

For comparison, see the tens of messages written by mentally incompetent and autistic people that are quoted in the book by Rabbi Yehudah Srevnik, *Secrets of the Soul,* and the booklets on communication which have recently come out: *Last Words Of The Last Generation* (2 booklets), *And I Will Put My Spirit In You, What Does The Soul Say?* among others. Many of Galia's messages also match up, nearly word for word, with the messages in these books.

This similarity leaves no doubt that the information expressed in their messages derives from the same Divine source. Hashem enables us to peek and see a bit of wondrous light that comes down to our world in order to light up the dark era.

Proof #4 — "Ima, Don't Marry Him!"

At the time that I became religious, I was a divorcee. I met a certain man and considered marrying him. In my second session with Galia (1/16/96), Galia wrote: "Ima, don't marry him. He is not a *yarei shamayim* [person who fears Heaven]. He's not for you. He'll cause you problems in becoming religious. He's not sincere. He'll bring you down."

She followed this with other specific, detailed points, which made me check into him more thoroughly than I had done. After doing this, I discovered to my great surprise that everything that Galia wrote was correct. If we were married, I would have fallen into the pit and at best managed to get divorced after a difficult divorce process. Or I might never have extricated myself. Thank G-d, the relationship ended.

I came to Galia and told her, "Galia, I want to thank you. You saved me. Everything you said about the man was correct."

Galia wrote to me: "Hashem sent you the message."

Via the facilitator Galia wrote me many messages about what was going on in my personal life. They were amazingly correct and precise. The facilitator could not have known the information Galia conveyed.

Proof #5 — "No Need For An Operation"

My sister went through a stomach operation but rather than improving, her condition got worse. She suffered from attacks of severe stomach cramps and high temperature. Since her surgeon had gone abroad, my sister consulted three top specialists. All of them were resolute that there was no alternative but to perform an additional operation to treat the infection and complications.

I told Galia about my sister. Galia wrote on Friday, 11/21/97:

> **Galia:** "Ima, in a short time the whole illness will disappear as though it never existed. In the meantime, she is atoning for her sins, because suffering purifies the soul to a great extent. Ima, she'll get out of it all very soon and there will be no need for any operation. Her doctor will locate the problem and treat her for it."
>
> **Ima:** The doctor who operated on her?
>
> **Galia:** Yes, he will know how to solve the problem. Because that's how Heaven has planned it all.

My sister, of course, had serious doubts about Galia's pronouncement. After all, three specialists had declared that she must undergo a further operation. She still has the doctors' written opinions testifying to this.

On Sunday, 11/23/97, the surgeon came back from abroad and my sister went to him at Wolfson Hospital in Cholon, prepared physically and psychologically for an operation.

To the surprise of us all, the surgeon decided to apply a simple external treatment which, sure enough, solved the problem. The surgeon said there was no need for an operation! My astounded sister, who was not religious and had been a policewoman with the Israeli Police Force, undertook to observe *Shabbos*.

Praise to Hashem, Healer of All Flesh and the Worker of Wonders.

Proof #6 — Her Expressions, Reactions And Gestures

Galia's facial expressions and gestures fit in with the content of the message she passes on and show that she understands what she is saying.

Galia is a good girl, pleasant and easygoing, who smiles a lot. If in a session Galia relays sad or painful messages (mainly, her messages to the Jewish people) she cries with tears the entire time that she is conveying the message. In all her other messages, on any other issue, she does not cry. Sometimes she laughs and makes sounds and gestures of happiness when delivering joyous messages.

After I produced a tape of my personal story of Galia, I played it to her. Galia started crying terribly without letup, really heart-breaking sobs. I asked Galia why she was crying, and she answered, "I don't like listening to unhappy things." (The tape starts with me describing all the torment we went through with Galia: all the times she passed out, running to hospital, the treatments, the sadness, and the pain, the nights we didn't sleep.) I immediately stopped playing the tape and she slowly calmed down.

Proof #7 — Knows The Contents Of My Shoulder Bag

In one of the early sessions, I asked Galia through a facilitator, "When I came to see you yesterday, what was inside my shoulder bag?" Galia pointed and wrote out on the board, "A *megillah* [scroll]."

That was correct. I was carrying with me a *Megillas Esther* [Scroll of Esther]. The facilitator assisting the session could not have known this.

Proof #8 — How Was It On Shabbos?

On Sunday, 4/21/96, Galia wrote to me via the facilitator, "Ima, you were so good to me on *Shabbos*. All the feeling you had. You were so happy. I love you so much. You're closer to the truth. In your heart, you are getting very near to Hashem and His truth. And the atmosphere of the home on *Shabbos* — you are careful about what is in truth permissible and forbidden. Even though it is difficult for you, you are progressing. And even if you are not always ready to make some change, I know that in the end you will change completely."

The facilitatior did not know that Galia had been home with me for *Shabbos*.

Galia also noted that I would change completely. This is what occurred. I changed completely.

Proof #9 — No Need For A Gas Mask

Everything that Galia wrote about the Gulf War and its effect on Israel proved correct. The messages appear in the first two Hebrew editions of *Galia*.

> **Ima:** Galia, I've brought you a mask with a pump and I've checked that everything works OK. What do you say — are we going to need these masks?
>
> **Galia:** Ima, we won't need any mask now. They are testing us in Heaven. (So it was. Saddam did not fire missiles with chemical warheads at Israel, and Israelis had no need for gas masks.)
>
> In December 1989, the UN forces launched an initial aerial attack against Iraq. I told Galia about it.
>
> **Ima:** Operation Desert Fox has started. America has started bombing Iraq. What do you say about it?
>
> **Galia:** Don't get tense over the American bombing in the Gulf. They'll stop in a couple of days. (That is in fact what happened.) This is just an initial show of force, to show and frighten them. The real bombing hasn't started.

Proof #10 — Interviews In The Media

In a message which was featured in the second book, *Good-bye to Galia?!?*, Galia wrote that the media would contact me for interviews.

It's amazing how all the predictions of Galia came true. Since publication of the book, I have appeared on Israeli Television Channel 2 and in a multi-page feature in *Kol Bo*, the major Northern Israeli weekly.

The Television Interview
    On Tuesday, 12/21/99, exactly as Galia wrote, I appeared live on Channel 2, on the popular show, *Avraham*

and Yaakov, hosted by the renowned TV personalities, Avri Gilad and Kobi Midan. During prime time, in front of a million viewers, I spoke for a quarter of an hour about the communication sessions with Galia, the messages, and the books. There was also a short clip of a session with Galia. Wonder of wonders — it was all exactly as Galia had noted beforehand.

The Press Feature

Kol Bo, a Haifa and North Israel newspaper with a distribution of hundreds of thousands, ran a 4-page feature with extensive descriptions and photos in its weekly edition of January 21, 2000. The feature spoke about Galia and FC. Galia had informed me in advance that this interview would take place.

Part 2

Galia's
Communications

Chapter Four:
The Life of the Soul

Ima, my name, גליה, says everything.
It declares what my character is
and my role in this world.
To reveal (גל) the word of Hashem (י-ה).

Chapter Four

❧ *The World of the Soul*

Ima: When does the soul enter the body? Is it before birth?

Galia: It enters the body at the moment the child is formed.

Ima: Do souls sleep at night?

Galia: No.

Ima: Galia, does my soul also know things?

Galia: Every Jewish soul knows everything.

Ima: Can you communicate with my soul?

Galia: Yes, and many times you have felt me doing this.

Ima: You mean what I felt a few days ago as though we were both floating in the skies together?

Galia: Right!

Ima: Does the soul get old?

Galia: No.

Ima: Do souls ever get ill?

Galia: There are soul diseases. These are spiritual diseases of the mind and heart for which one needs *tikun*.

Ima: Can the souls of *tzadikim* in *Gan Eden* get ill?

Galia: No.

Ima: What makes a soul more wise or less wise?

Galia: What makes his soul wise is if he is a servant of Hashem; then his soul will be healthy and whole and capable of enjoying the holy light. If he is a *tzadik* and a servant of Hashem in this world, then he will get to a wonderful place in the next world.

Ima: What's this holy light? Are you allowed to say?

Galia: Hashem.

Ima: What happens in Heaven to the soul of one who did not accept the yoke of the kingdom of Heaven? Does it remain deficient?

Galia: It will disappear completely.

Ima: Galia, how and why does my having done *teshuva* help you?

Galia: Because our souls are linked and therefore, if you are not whole then I am not whole.

Ima: After death does the soul have the same character that it had when it was alive?

Galia: Sure. Ima, the soul does not have senses like a living person, but it feels everything and knows everything and sees and hears everything.

Ima: Do you have freedom of thought? Can you think and do what you want?

Galia: I am a person too. I have a certain intelligence, and with that intelligence, I have free choice. But it's not wide-ranging. It's not possible for me to know what I want, because Heaven decides what I may know and say and nothing depends on me. The soul tells the body what to do, but the body is limited and cannot do what the soul tells it because it is material and the soul is spiritual. All the same, souls do not have the ability to make independent decisions. Everything is dictated to it by Heaven. I am like a soul bound to the will of Heaven.

Ima: Do you communicate with other souls?

Galia: I am never alone. Sometimes I communicate with children even if they are far off. The soul is not limited by distance at all.

Ima: Is the soul alone by itself in Heaven?

Galia: No. It's together with angels.

Ima: When a man comes to this world and completes his *tikun*, does he become a *tzadik*?

Galia: Ima, it's not like that. Even if he completes his *tikun*, he is not exactly a *tzadik*, but a soul which has consummated itself. There are souls which have consummated themselves, but aren't *tzadikim*.

Ima: Where will they be in Heaven?

Galia: They will get to enter *Gan Eden* but they will not be in the area of the *tzadikim*. It's all a matter of the *zechus* which each soul has.

Ima: You said that in the next world, there is only harmony. There is no loneliness and isolation. But in the next world you go on living with the same souls who lived in this world, since in the end, everyone passes on to the next world. So how do they suddenly change into such good and pleasant people?

Galia: Ima, you pass on to live with those who are compatible with the particular soul. Every soul lives with the souls with which they are compatible. This does not always happen in this world because this world is for a person's *tikun*.

Ima: Does a person also have a mother and father in the next world or is it only in this world?

Galia: Ima, in the next world, Hashem is the only father any of us have. Only in this world is there such a thing as mother and father. There they are not one's mother and father. There they are souls like all of us and there is no difference. It is just the opposite. Sometimes, the child is made up of a bigger soul than his father.

✤ The Soul and Its Tikun

Ima: If Heaven tells the soul what it's expected to do in this world to fulfill its purpose here, and the soul wants to go ahead and do it, but the body doesn't listen to it — how can it achieve its *tikun*, if the body doesn't listen to it?

Galia: Ima, the soul can fulfill its mission because it manipulates the body. Even if it doesn't control it physically, it directs its thoughts towards its *tikun*. Everything comes from the brain, and the brain tells the body what to do, and then the body does it. That's how the soul controls the body and tells it what to do.

Ima: What about the brain of a person with mental incompetence? His brain does not tell its body anything, because it does not have enough intelligence to tell the body anything.

Galia: Ima, then its *tikun* is achieved mainly through its suffering.

Ima: Galia, is your soul more sensitive that that of a person who is unaware of his soul? Could it be that you've got a very sensitive soul? You cry when you hear sad things. Are all souls so sensitive like that?

Galia: Ima, my soul is more sensitive than that of a normal person and there are other souls like mine which are more sensitive.

Ima: Is it good to be sensitive or not? Don't sensitive people just get hurt?

Galia: Ima, it is good only in Heaven, after life. Then the spiritually sensitive souls are bigger receptors for experiencing the pleasures of the eternal and unlimited. They are big receptacles for all the divine bounty which awaits us in our eternal life.

Ima: Who tells you what to say?

Galia: Ima, a *bas kol,* the voice of Heaven, tells me what to tell you.

Ima: Galia, I wanted to tell you that after I asked someone for an apology, she rang me up on her own initiative, and this made me very happy because that's a sign that there is room for forgiveness in people's hearts.

Galia: I am very happy, Ima. It's forbidden for a person to have someone who hasn't forgiven him for something, because in Heaven, he will be put on trial over this. If everybody forgave him in this world, he is not tried for this. It's easier for the soul in the court of Heaven when everyone has forgiven him. Otherwise it suffers a great deal in Heaven.

Ima: All in all, you live in this world seventy or eighty years. Could it be that everything you do here is eternal? It seems to me that life is very short in comparison with all the limitless *shefa* which you get afterwards for eternity.

Galia: Correct, Ima. This is the kindness which Hashem shows us and we don't grasp how this short life gives us the opportunity to have eternal joy.

Ima: Is the soul of a dead person allowed to see its relatives who are alive in this world and assist them? Does it know what's happening in their lives?

Galia: The soul of someone who died can see and find out everything about its relatives. If it has the *zechus*, it can help them. It depends on the *zechuyos* of the particular soul. But it is not allowed to communicate with them. Sometimes it gets permission to appear in a dream.

Ima: What in fact is the *yetzer hatov* – the good will and the *yetzer hora* – the evil will? Could it be that the soul is made up of two forces, good and evil, and it has to overcome the evil and act in accordance with the good?

Galia: Ima, these are in fact powerful spiritual forces which everyone has, and during his life, he has to subdue and overcome the evil in favor of the good. These two forces vie with each constantly, until the person succeeds in subduing evil or succumbing to it. Obviously, the preferred objective is to overcome it.

Ima: How do you explain the fact that you love all the Jewish people so much and worry about them as much as you do?

Galia: Ima, I am part of the collective soul of the Jewish people and that is the explanation of my love for the people. If there is something wrong with a part of the body, it affects the whole body. I am part of the soul of the Jewish people and if something has gone wrong, then I am in pain.

Ima: How does it come to be that a certain person starts to think about the world around him and discover the light and the truth and do *teshuva*, while it happens to someone else at a different age and time, if at all? How is it that one person has the *zechus* to do *teshuva* while someone else doesn't?

Galia: That is a *zechus* which that particular soul has, be it *zechus avos* or a *zechus* from a previous life. For some the *zechus* is realized in this world.

Ima: I heard a certain rabbi on the radio who said that a man comes to this world with the form and appearance necessary for him to complete his *tikun* in this world. What's your opinion?

Galia: Ima, a person comes to the world in the form he needs for the *tikun* that he has to acheive. He is equipped and supplied appropriately for his *tikun*, so he can achieve it without the hindrance of being disadvantaged. Whether or not he completes that *tikun* is entirely up to him.

Ima: Once you told me that you came as a *gilgul* to this world just because of me, to get me to do *teshuva*. If you didn't have to get me to do *teshuva*, would you not have come in a *gilgul*?

Galia: I came to the world as a *gilgul* only because of you, because I really wanted to get you to do *teshuva*. I could have been rectified in Heaven and in *Gehinom*; I did not have to come here. But I knew I would succeed with you. So I was happy to come, and in doing so, in your *zechus*, I have succeeded in adding to my *zechuyos*. That really gives me delirious pleasure because I have a *zechus* in everything you do. Someone who gets a person to do *teshuva* gets all his *zechuyos* too. The souls here rectify the sum total of the collective and while at the same time rectifying its own individual soul.

Ima: When the soul gets to Heaven, does it recognize all its family members who have lived hundreds, even thousands, of years ago?

Galia: Ima, the soul recognizes everyone. The souls recognize everyone from every generation. It's no problem. Every soul in Heaven identifies everyone and is happy to meet them.

Ima: What happens when a man with the spiritual ability of a *tzadik* comes to the world and goes down a spiritual level instead of increasing his spiritual level during his lifetime? When he gets to Heaven, do they give him another opportunity to come here to this world and make good of the situation in order for him to go up a level again or does he stay on his low level?

Galia: Ima, he can't come back every time. He will then forever remain at the last level he was at, here in this world. There is no one who knows whether he will come back to this world or not. Everyone has to make a maximum effort as though it's his last time here, because it's possible that it is his last time here. In Heaven, no one is deprived of anything. It's just painful for the souls who could have done much more in this world and make do with only a little.

Ima: Galia, you tell me that I succeeded because my sources are in Torah, *mitzvos* and *ma'asim tovim*. That reminds me that Torah, *mitzvos* and *ma'asim tovim* is exactly what you came to rectify in this *gilgul*, because you didn't give your children a proper education in those things. Therefore since I, due to you, fulfill these *mitzvos*, is it therefore now reckoned as though you gave your children a proper education in Torah, *mitzvos* and *ma'asim tovim*?

Galia: My dear mother, that's very true. That's exactly what my *tikun* is, that you got to do *mitzvos* and *ma'asim tovim* — that which I had failed to impart to my children in my last *gilgul*.

Ima: Galia, I don't know how you educated the rest of your children, but my father *zichrono levracha* who was your son in your last *gilgul*, was a *tzadik*, honest and decent, and you yourself said he is in *Gan Eden*. So in what way did you not bring up your children properly? Or is it that they are just strict with *tzadikim*?

Galia: Ima, both those views are correct. Hashem is truth and His judgment is perfect truth and justice. But *tzadikim* are submitted to very exacting judgment based on their capability because *tzadikim* have much higher capabilities than other people.

Ima: What are you allowed to say about your other half?

[*In* Kabala, *every soul is divided into two halves and the halves are sent to the world where they may reunite as man and wife. Ultimately, they reunite in the next world.*]

Galia: My other half is waiting for me in Heaven. Ima, no one lives for eternity and at a certain time I will return to my place of permanence. There my soul won't feel the heaviness of material substance. It is there that I will be rejoined with my other half.

Ima: Why are you ending your *tikun* with the completion of my book about you? There are people with autism and mental incompetence whom people have written about, and published their writings in Rabbi Srevnik's book, and they are not ending their *tikun* with this.

Galia: Ima, each one has his own *tikun*.

Ima: You often say that one has to restore the soul, and that suffering helps to repair it. What do you mean by "to consummate the soul"? Does the soul lack something like a foot or a hand?

Galia: Ima, that's exactly it — but spiritually! It's missing a part of its source because of its sins. What each person is missing depends on the person himself based on what he's done. But sometimes a soul is missing many parts; and by suffering and anguish and through the observance of studying Torah and the performance of *mitzvos* in this world, the parts are then restored.

Ima: Galia, you said that it's important for a person not to get attached to material things because it's hard for the person who is attached to material things to die, since in the spiritual world, he suffers over the material things he misses. Is it harder for rich people to die?

Galia: It's hard for a person to give up on material things. It's very hard for rich people to leave this world. The fact that they are rich is also part of their *tikun*. When a rich man gets to Heaven, he sees that there you don't need all the money or any material property.

Ima: Can souls in Heaven argue or get angry with each other?

Galia: *Chas ve'shalom!* Ima, there's no evil will in the next world. Everything is good, pleasant and beautiful. No one gets angry and there are no arguments.

Ima: Galia, when a man comes to this world, Heaven knows beforehand if he's going to do *teshuva* and fulfill his mission or not. So why do they send people to this world who they know will not do *teshuva*?

Galia: My dear Ima, even so, they give every soul the opportunity to come to this world and put everything right. It's better for every human being to achieve his *tikun* when he is in the clothes of the material world, because that's the best and easiest *tikun*.

Ima: That's called easy? Some people go through terrible suffering in this world.

Galia: Even when it's hard to understand why, it's for the good. It's hard to explain. The worst form of suffering is actually outside the body and not inside the body because the soul is given the means to feel almost limitless suffering. Ima, it's hard to explain spiritual things to you. Since you exist in material form, you do not have the tools to understand. Fortunate are those who have the *zechus* to perform *mitzvos* and enjoy the next world dressed in the royal clothes they prepared for themselves in this world.

Ima: What happens to the soul of a person whose children have not done *teshuva*?

Galia: If she is guilty because she did not educate her children, her shame is simply awful. But if someone did educate them in Torah and *mitzvos* and they went rotten, they have to render an account for themselves.

Ima: Is there no need to be sad over a person who feared Heaven, who died?

Galia: If somebody was known to have good *midos* and was a fine person, and because of his deeds he ranked as a *tzadik*, then one should only be slightly sad for him. For him, abandoning the material for the spiritual is a great joy. This is the reason for the celebrations held on the anniversaries of the deaths of *tzadikim*. People share in their joy that they rose to high spiritual levels in their lives which give them life in the next world.

Ima: Can you explain to me the role of those who experience clinical death? What purpose does it serve?

Galia: Ima, they have a very important role — to relate what they saw to strengthen the faith of the listener. Someone who has gone through this knows that he has been given an extension of life in order to do *teshuva* and to rectify what he has damaged. It's like a last warning before being sent to live a further life in this world or receiving a hard punishment.

Ima: When the soul arrives in the next world, who shows it the way in the High worlds? How does it know where to go?

Galia: Ima, every soul is received by high angels, holy serving angels, if it has the *zechus*. If it is the soul of a *tzadik,* then other *tzadikim* come to greet it with great joy and happiness to show it the place prepared for it in Heaven.

Ima: Do evil spirits come to a soul after death?

Galia: They are not allowed to get near *tzadikim*. Evil spirits torment the souls of evil people who have sinned and cleanse them of the impurity of their sins.

Ima: Is there a concept of time in the next world?

Galia: Time is a different concept in the next world than it is in this world. In the spiritual world one has, as it were, all the time in the world.

Ima: Maybe you can tell me how Moshe *Rabbeinu* succeeded in reaching such mighty spiritual levels? Or was it that from the outset he had an ability and mighty spiritual potential that hardly anyone has?

Galia: Ima, Moshe *Rabbeinu* had massive spiritual ability; but he also actualized this ability. This is why a person should exert himself more and more and try as much as he can. That's the only way he can know if he has the ability to do more. Every soul will have to render account for every cell which could have functioned here in this world in the time given it and did nothing. The soul is only happy if it achieved the goal that it was sent to accomplish. If it did not succeed in its assignment, it's in mourning and it is ashamed. That's the hardest Gehinom.

Ima: Are even very clever people limited in comparison with their souls?

Galia: Yes Ima. Compared to the soul, the mind is like some primitive invention. It is the soul that is all-wise. Everything is spiritual and beyond our small understanding and limited abilities of perception in this world of falsity. The most intelligent person in the world is extremely primitive in contrast to the enlightened soul. Ima, intelligence is one thing and souls are something else completely. The mind is built in a very limited form.

✤ In The Court Of Heaven

Ima: Are all souls tried in the court of Heaven – in the *Beis Din Shel Ma'alah*?

Galia: Yes. They check and see the soul's *zechuyos* and *chovos* and it receives reward and punishment according to what it deserves so that it will not be deprived of whatever reward it is due.

Ima: Is every soul required to go before the court of Heaven?

Galia: Sure, Ima. Otherwise, how will the court of Heaven know what it deserves if it doesn't check?

Ima: Is it frightening to be tried in the court of Heaven?

Galia: Ima, it's terrible. The soul shakes like a leaf. It's so afraid of the holiness that it cannot open its mouth. Then all the *mitzvos* it did in this world appear and plead for it, because the soul is unable to do anything for itself. Only its deeds can act on its behalf.

Ima: Can the soul not plead for itself in front of the court of Heaven, or speak up and say anything for itself?

Galia: It cannot open its mouth due to its terrible fear. It has to be helped by advocates.

Ima: Who can act as an advocate for it? Just its *mitzvos* or can *tzadikim* also plead for it?

Galia: Ima, all its *mitzvos* appear before it and obviously all its sins, and that's how they try it in the court of Heaven.

Ima: It's shocking and frightening. What can you do to make the trial process easier? What can you do beforehand to make it less frightening?

Galia: The only means in this world is Torah and *mitzvos*. Then the procedure in the Court of Heaven is easier to cope with. In heaven it is very unfortunate for those who don't fulfill the Torah and *mitzvos*. The pain of their soul is so sharp and so deep that you can't even describe it with words.

Ima: Galia, does the court of Heaven judge leniently and take things into account or does it judge only with exactitude, without taking anything into account?

Galia: Ima, if someone's deeds were worthy and he is a *tzadik,* and he stumbled and fell and committed a sin only on a few occasions, but regretted it and did *teshuva* and took extra caution from then on — only then do they judge him leniently. But all those who throw off the yoke and deny Hashem and the Torah are judged with great strictness, especially those who take the law into their own hands and commit suicide or murder.

Ima: Someone once asked me, "Why do you communicate with your daughter? Hidden affairs are the business of G-d and apparent matters are ours." What am I to say to that?

Galia: Ima, tell them that they don't understand this concept because if they did, they would not talk like that.

There are revelations of the truth from the high worlds which are done on a number of levels, and one of them is communication with the mentally incompetent. There are people who have all kinds of revelations and visions. The *tzadikim* of our generation have the *zechus* to know things which were hidden for hundreds of years. Now, as the time gets nearer to the *geula*, Hashem reveals them to us because before the day of the great and terrible name, Hashem reveals to us from Heaven a lot of truths which will progressively increase and grow.

So these things are not closed secrets which are forbidden to delve into. These are revelations which Hashem is revealing, and changing from closed secrets to revelations, for us. We are fortunate to see the Divine Truth which is starting to be revealed in our world and is carving its way in this world of falsity.

Ima: Galia, when you say that the way Hashem runs the world is starting to be revealed, that is very exciting to me. Does that mean that Hashem is not hiding His face from us any longer?

Galia: Correct, Ima. What's happening in our generation is very exciting. If only everyone would open his eyes to see this happiness which is coming down to the world, that Hashem loves us so much and is starting a new form of divine conduct with us, in the form of *gilui panim* – a revealed face. My dear Ima, I am happy to tell you that the era of the *hester panim* — the era of His hidden face — is passing from the world.

Ima: What a wonderful message, *baruch Hashem!* Galia, I wanted to ask you, before I pass on the material to the rabbi to be checked — are there things which may not be written in the book?

Galia: Ima, everything I have said to you is all right, and people are allowed to know all this. But everything must be checked by your rabbi. Everything which your rabbi approves of is accepted in Heaven. The main thing is not to be tempted into doing things on your own without being checked.

Hashem has mercy on his beloved Jewish people and reveals to them secrets of the Torah — to anyone who wants — because Hashem wants to release us from our troubles right away and, in His goodness, renew this world. Everything is from Heaven, the whole need to speak about the revelations of the truth from the high worlds which has been revealed to us recently. Heaven is arranging things to make the *geula* easier for us. We have to give thanks to the Creator of the World who is helping us to open our sealed eyes and think about what's going on around us.We must understand that we, the beloved Jewish people, must fulfill the *mitzvos* of Hashem without any conditions or reservations. We must serve Him with great love, because He is gracious and merciful, with a fantastic love, and he protects us and directs us all the time. All we have to do is think.

Ima, you cry over the people who were killed by terrorists and I cry over the Jewish people from *Adam Harishon* to now and beyond. The world is rapidly progressing to its end. The end is the beginning of a new world, a world of truth, not of falsity. But a lot of Jews still don't understand that, and I am worried.

Ima: Is everyone's *teshuva* accepted in Heaven?

Galia: Sure. Heaven accepts the true *teshuva* of all. The biggest *tzadik* is the one who controls his *yetzer hara* and does *teshuva* — not necessarily the person who doesn't have a *yetzer hora*. Getting people to do *teshuva* is considered one of the biggest *mitzvos* a man can do in this world. Right now, the defenses and *zechuyos* we have are not enough. We're just dependent on the *zechuyos* of the *tzadikim* who have died, and we, the living, do not have enough *zechuyos*. Ima, it helps me that you came to me today, because today I am extremely sad over my precious Jewish people. It's important to pray to Hashem, to cry to Him, and to ask Him to have mercy on His people.

✣ The Soul Of Adam Harishon

Ima: I wanted to ask you, Galia. Why are we to blame for the fact that *Adam Harishon* sinned and why have we suffered so much for thousands of years and generations? Why are we to blame for the sin that he committed?

Galia: Ima, *Adam Harishon* sinned with pure intentions, to rectify the world in a different way than it was when it was offered to him. It's hard for me to explain everything to you but you have to appreciate that we are also to blame because we are in fact part of the soul of *Adam Harishon*. We are not suffering because of him, but because of ourselves.

Ima: Your brother says that we are rectifying the sin of *Adam Harishon* and when we finish rectifying it, man will sin again and man will again have to go through thousands of years of history to rectify the sin. So what's the point of all the *tikun*, if we sin again?

Galia: He doesn't understand that Hashem made man as a continuation of perfection. Everything which has happened up until now is a divine process to bring man to the perfection which he lost in *Gan Eden*. When he reaches perfection again, Hashem will kill the evil will, and after the resurrection of the dead, at the end of these days, those who remain will reach true spiritual perfection.

Ima: Then man will no longer have freedom of choice?

Galia: Correct. He won't need it.

Ima: A certain rabbi asked whether ultimately all souls will combine and be in the body of *Adam Harishon* as he was created?

Galia: The object is to rectify the sin of *Adam Harishon*, to reach the merging of all the holy sparks, which together will be redeemed from their captivity, and achieve the goal of returning to being a part of the soul of *Adam Harishon*.

Ima: In my opinion, this world is very beautiful. It has trees, flowers, birds, fields, wonderful views, and the sun. Everything is extremely beautiful. It's just that the people in it aren't always beautiful, but it would seem that the world itself is very beautiful.

Galia: Ima, it's a wonderful world, but it will be perfect the way you imagine it only when *Mashiach* comes and all the *tikunim* are complete. The soul of *Adam Harishon* will again be complete. Everything will be different. It will be a wonderful world just as described in the religious works. There will be rivers of oil and rivers of wine, and everything will grow in a day. A little baby will be able to observe, look and see secrets of all the worlds. Everything will happen, Ima. And it will all happen soon. Ima, the end is getting very near. It's already here at the entrance. Our generation will *b'ezras Hashem* have the *zechus* to see mighty events and the fulfillment of the prophecies. We all have to become pure quickly. Only purification can enable us to receive the light which is so mighty and wonderful.

Ima: If before its descent to this world the soul in Heaven agreed to achieve its *tikun* and fulfill its mission here, why are there souls which do not achieve a *tikun* and complete their mission?

Galia: Ima, this world is a world full of personal desires and the *yetzer hora* constantly tries very hard to make a person fail. It's very difficult for the material body to cope with the *yetzer hora* which offers it so many material pleasures. It's extremely hard to overcome material cravings. Overcoming and subduing the *yetzer hora* is the *tikun* of the sin of *Adam Harishon*. Some people don't succeed and they become captives of the material and they have to do a further *tikun*.

Ima, everything changes all the time, depending on how far the soul succeeds in collecting sparks of holiness in its stay here. The amount of its success in its task in this world determines its place after its life and existence in the body. All those who are not sensible enough to fulfill their mission faithfully and are into materialism and influenced by the *tum'ah* which surrounds them and hides them in its shells — *klippos* — their souls are desperately unhappy. The pain they have from the failure to overcome the *yetzer hora* is eternally insufferable. You understand everything with the greatest possible clarity in the world of truth. So long as the candle is alight, you can achieve a *tikun*. But some people do not achieve a *tikun* while the candle is lit. They push everything off and the candle comes to an end, but not their *tikun*.

Chapter Five:
This World and the Next:
Gezairos and Geula

I believe ... in the coming of Mashiach,
and even though he is delayed,
I wait for him to come every day.

Maimonides

Chapter Five

❧ *Gan Eden And Gehinom*

Ima: Do *Gan Eden* and *Gehinom* exist?

Galia: That's not even a question.

Ima: Why? Is it forbidden to ask?

Galia: It's allowed. But it's clear — of course they exist!

Ima: I heard a rabbi who said you even have to have *zechus* to get into *Gehinom*. According to the rabbi, *Gehinom* is not a punishment. A man goes to *Gehinom* to cure his soul is like a man who enters the hospital, ready for all the suffering and pain necessary to cure him of his illness and enable him to function normally. What's your opinion about that?

Galia: Ima, that's all correct.

Ima: What is the *Kaf Hakela*? Are you allowed to tell me?

Galia: The *Kaf Hakela* is a place. What takes place there is similar to a game of tennis in which two angels of destruction shoot the soul of a sinner from one end of the world to the other. They give no rest to the soul. These are the worst sufferings for the person who has not been allowed to enter *Gehinom*. After a period in the *Kaf Hakela*, the length of which depends on his sins, he then enters into *Gehinom* and receives his *tikun* there. All this can be avoided if you keep the Torah and its *mitzvos*.

Ima: Do you have some advice as to how to be saved from *Gehinom*? What do you have to do in this world in order not to have to go to *Gehinom* at all?

Galia: You can be saved from *Gehinom* through the *zechus* of spreading Torah. Spreading Torah is not a person's obligation in this world but Heaven shows much kindness to the person who spreads Torah because he is helping other people for the sake of Heaven.

Ima: Is spreading Torah the formula, or are there other ways also to be saved from *Gehinom*?

Galia: Ima, all our work in this world is in order not to need additional cleansing before one's entrance into *Gan Eden*.

Ima: Are all the people in Heaven *tzadikim*?

Galia: It is possible that they were once wicked men who then did *teshuva*, but then they are forever thought of as *tzadikim*.

Ima: I heard a rabbi say that after they die, wicked people are shown all the sins they have done during their lives and that they are so ashamed of themselves, they don't even wait until they are thrown into *Gehinom,* but throw themselves in instead.

Galia: That's what happens to those wicked people who have wasted their whole lives with idle pursuits and sinning instead of performing *mitzvos* and being honest with Hashem.

Ima: I heard that the rabbi said that *Gan Eden* is in fact in this world, here, and that after mankind purifies its soul and its body, *Gan Eden* will then be in this world.

Galia: One can have some experience of *Gan Eden* here, but there is also a higher *Gan Eden* where the *tzadikim* sit with their crowns are on their heads and they bask in the radiance of the *Shechina.*

Ima: What's easier for the soul — to go to *Gehinom* or to come back to this world?

Galia: Both are difficult for it. Because even in this world there are places which do not receive the holy light, even though there are also places which are filled with the holy light without limit.

✤ *This World And The Next World*

Ima: They say that in Heaven, in *Gan Eden,* there are spiritual trees, spiritual rivers and streams, and spiritual fruits. Is everything spiritual there?

Galia: Ima, it's true that Heaven has everything. But everything there is spiritual, not like the material existence in this world. You cannot picture the limitless *shefa* that is there.

Ima: Is the next world blurred, cloudy and unclear like in a dream? Or is it sharp and clear like life in this world?

Galia: Ima, the only cloudiness and confusion that exist are here in this world, the world of falsity. The next world is the ultimate clarity. The next world is clear, very clear and bright. It's not like in a dream. It's much clearer than our reality here.

Ima: After dying, after one hundred and twenty years, will everyone know all the answers to all the questions?

Galia: In the next world, there are answers to all the questions people can possibly have. There are no unanswered questions there. Everyone will know the truth in the next world, nothing is hidden there. Everything is clear, revealed and known. In this world, the truth is hidden because that's how everything is directed from Heaven — so that we won't know everything, and we can remain with free choice and arrive at the truth only through our sheer will.

Ima: Tell me, Galia, is there loneliness and isolation in the next world like in this world?

Galia: Ima, there's no such thing there. That's only in this world. In the next world, everyone lives in brotherhood and perfect harmony.

Ima: My friend Chaya told me that she read a book that describes what happens when the soul reaches Heaven. It sees that it will be held on some particular level on which it will remain for eternity, and it is extremely sad over the fact that it did not serve Hashem harder in this world, losing the opportunity to reach higher levels. The soul has great sadness and terrible anguish because it knows that this is the end of its progress and that for eternity it will never be able to rise higher.

Galia: Ima, that's very correct because every soul is awarded according to the action of his person when he is in this world. It's worth a person's while to put a lot of effort in [mitzvos] even if it is extremely difficult for him. We didn't come to this world just to enjoy ourselves. We came here to work hard and toil, to obtain our spiritual pleasures through hard work.

Ima: The Torah shows us the way in this world. It teaches us how to behave, to fulfill *mitzvos* and live in it. So how does it apply to the next world, which is spiritual and where, according to my understanding, you don't perform *mitzvos*?

Galia: Ima, our holy Torah is for all the worlds and it is beyond our ability to understand this with the limited tools of the mind. In the world of truth, you get other tools of understanding and knowledge which man does not have here in this world. But they are faculties which the soul has and can only be implemented in the higher worlds.

Ima: Galia, does everyone in Heaven have his own home or private area which belongs to him exclusively, like in this world?

Galia: Ima, everyone in Heaven has his own exclusive area meant only for him. It all depends on the *zechus* of his *ma'asim tovim* in this world and the *zechuyos* he accumulated here. For every *mitzva*, brick upon brick is built, based on what he deserves.

Ima: Does the soul in the next world co-exist with its other half?

Galia: Ima, don't worry. Every soul exists with its other half according to its *zechuyos*. If it has many *zechuyos* then it lives in supernal bliss and with its other half the entire time. However, if a person didn't trouble himself enough in this world and just went looking for pleasures and just got what he could from people and did not give to them anything, he will not be with his other half all the time in Heaven, but only a little bit. His soul will not have the *zechus* of perfect happiness. Hashem gives the *tzadikim* who strive for the sake of Heaven daily the *zechus* of being with their other halves forever.

Ima: It is said that a man who didn't purify himself in this world is purified in Heaven. So why can't every soul be purified in Heaven? Why are souls sent here when they can be purified there?

Galia: Ima, it's not like that. This world has more functions than purifying souls. The best thing for you to do is to concentrate on action, *mitzvos* and *ma'asim tovim*. Because we have no time and the world passes quicky like a shadow.

Ima: Will you be handicapped in the next world?

Galia: Ima, in the next world, there are no handicapped. They are only here for *tikun*. The people who are handicapped and pathetic in the next world are the ones who did not get to go into *Gan Eden* and they still wander around or are in *Gehinom*. They are the real handicapped. They are the unfortunate people.

Galia: In the next world, it is not possible to rectify things as easily as it is in this world. *Teshuva* has a mighty power. *Teshuva* is a terrific gift that we have had the *zechus* to receive. *Teshuva* gets to the Throne of Glory.

✤ *Resurrection Of The Dead*

Ima: How do you explain that the whole purpose of this world is for a man to prepare himself for the next world? That the whole purpose of this world is the next world, and then at the time of the resurrection of the dead, everyone will then return and live here in this world. Isn't that a contradiction?

Galia: Ima, there is the next world, which is the world one hopes to go to after one dies and you have to work hard to receive *zechuyos* to merit it. Then there is the world of the resurrection of the dead, which is another world. Those who deserve it will come here again to live in a perfected world, because after the resurrection of the dead, this world will be like *Gan Eden*.

Ima: Galia, what do we have to do to deserve resurrection? I have heard that even the righteous gentiles of the world will rise at the resurrection.

Galia: All of us shall rise at the resurrection and to do so we must accept the yoke of Torah and *mitzvos*; otherwise we shall not rise. Of the gentiles, only those who observe the seven Noahide Laws will rise.

Ima: Does it make any difference to the body or the soul where the body is buried after death, whether in Israel, Jerusalem or the rest of Israel?

Galia: Ima, the best thing for the soul is for its body to be buried in the holy city of Jerusalem. There it will be among the first to rise. Afterwards, the dead of the dust of the land of Israel will rise. Then the *tzadikim* of the Jewish people buried in the rest of the world will rise. Right at the end, the righteous of the gentiles will also rise.

Ima: Are you allowed to tell me which body will rise at the resurrection of the dead? Is it the body which did the final *tikun*?

Galia: Ima, I am not allowed to answer that despite the fact that I have a clear answer. If it was permitted to tell, then everyone would have found out a long time ago.

Ima: Galia, I have the feeling that everybody will have to die before the resurrection of the dead. And only after everyone dies will the resurrection of the dead take place, and then death will no longer exist. It seems to me that only the suffering of death of all men on earth will rectify the sin of Adam. I form this conclusion from the fact that all the generations had *tzadikim* who died because of the decree on Adam and not because of any sin they did. Yishai — King David's father, Amram, Binyamin and Calev, David's son, were perfect *tzadikim* whom the *yetzer hora* never influenced, and they still died. What's your opinion? Will everyone have to die before the resurrection of the dead?

Galia: I am not allowed to tell you. Even if you study Torah hard and look for an answer to this question, you still won't find it. The answer will come when it must descend to the world, and then, at the right time, people will know the answers to these questions.

Ima: Do you know?

Galia: Ima, I know everything, but I am not allowed to tell you everything.

✣ *Gezairos And Geula*

Galia: Ima, don't wait, the ending of the exile for the Jewish people is imminent and you have to complete your *teshuva,* because there's no time. Ima, I worry about you so much. There's a bitter *gezaira* that's been made by Heaven to inflict disaster on the Jewish nation. You have to pray and do *teshuva.* Hashem is making Heaven's reckoning and issuing many warnings. Hashem is a perfect judge. Those who do not accept the yoke of Heaven before the *geula* may not be rewarded with eternal life.

Ima: Galia, when I ask you a question, who tells you what to say? How do you know what to tell me?

Galia: Ima, when you ask me a question, at the same moment a voice emanates from Heaven and tells me what to tell you.

Ima, I'm terribly afraid for the Jews; a major portion of them are asleep. The situation is so difficult for the Jewish people and soon it will become much more difficult. Only the loving G-d can save us. Ima, you have to do everything the right way. The word of Hashem is law. It's an extremely difficult time for the Jewish people. Jews are blind. They don't see the simple truth that the Master Of The World is the one who decides. Anyone can see that our Father In Heaven cannot let his children go on like this. Hashem sends all kinds of signs to help us see the truth. But most people don't understand. Unless there's danger and fear, we don't really accept the yoke of Heaven. I have to tell you that I am extremely worried. We are in grave danger, spiritual danger. But most of us don't understand, or seem to understand that.

Ima: What is spiritual danger? Could a situation occur in which Hashem wipes out the Jewish people for not listening to His voice?

Galia: The entire world, and particularly the Jews, are in spiritual danger today. There are *tzadikim*. But bit by bit we are using up their *zechuyos*. We have no other source aside from our *teshuva*. It's very frightening. Ima, Hashem won't wipe out the whole nation. But there can be a situation in which He has to purify the nation.

Ima: What do we have to do to improve the situation?

Galia: *Teshuva*. A man has to break the *klippa* — the shell of this world — and take his life apart and extract the spiritual impurity from it. Only after this process can he then put himself together as a new man. It involves a lot of suffering. People want it easy and they want to feel good and happy, but there is no other way to bring the salvation. Either Hashem brings it or we do. A big part of the nation is fast asleep and they have to wake up so that there will be someone to welcome *Mashiach* when he comes, *b'ezras Hashem*. Ima, we are definitely in the middle of a very great era for the Jewish people and mankind in general. We are at the point of seeing grand, shattering revelations in our time. People feel this in their souls and know that something is going to happen, but they can't exactly define it for themselves. And no one knows when the end will be.

Ima: How can a person become less afraid of the hard times to come? How can the severe *gezairos* be cancelled?

Galia: Through *teshuva*, prayer, and charity and loving every Jew. Helping people as much as possible is the key. You can help a person both through physical assistance and financial assistance. Heaven is kind to the one who is kind to others.

Ima: Does G-d forgive the person who does *teshuva* for all he did before he did *teshuva*?

Galia: If a man does true *teshuva*, out of love for G-d, then his sins become *zechuyos*. But if a man does *teshuva* because he's afraid, and not because he entirely wants to, like a sick man who is about to die but just wants his life to be saved, then it's a different story. It depends on the case. Heavens accepts the true *teshuva* of everyone.

Ima: How is it possible to cancel the *gezairos* or to lessen their severity?

Galia: It is possible only if all the Jews in the land do a massive *teshuva*.

Ima: Galia, there is a mass *teshuva* going on now. Isn't that considered a "mass teshuva"?

Galia: Ima, it's still not a mass *teshuva*. It's in the right direction but it's not enough. All the same, Heaven is excited over the *ma'asim tovim* that put the Jewish people in a good light, contributing to its defense in these mixed-up days.

Ima: Does this religious revival mean Heaven will not issue any more harsh decrees against the Jewish people?

Galia: Ima, I cannot say that it cancels everything. But the fact that there is this big revival helps us so much, and it reduces a great many of the impending disasters.

Ima: What about children and their ability to cancel the bad *gezairos* which we are facing?

Galia: "The fathers have eaten sour grapes," (*Yirmiyahu* 31:28) but the prayers of children in the *cheder* can cancel the disasters with the vapor of their mouths. In fact, children, through their suffering, atone for the sins of their fathers.

Dear Ima, you have to understand that the forces of evil know specifically that this is the end for them. Therefore, like a wounded animal, they are trying to win out with the last of their strengths. These forces are trying to bring more people to evil, through violence between individuals and a general violence among the nations of the world. We must preserve our path in holiness and do the will of Heaven. We must not respond to the *yetzer hora* who comes from the forces of evil to lure our thoughts to sin.

Ima: Why does everyone have to suffer from the difficult situation? Why are those who have already woken up also to blame?

Galia: Ima, we, the Jewish nation, are all judged as a unit because we are one big soul. If one part of the body hurts, the whole body hurts. Ima, I watch, see and hear the *bas kol* resounding in Heaven and announcing what is going to happen. I can only tell you the slightest part of what I see, but it will be terrible if the *gezaira* is not cancelled. Tell everyone that they should make the maximum possible effort to observe *mitzvos*, pray, and study Torah a great deal, because all of this can cancel these impending *gezairos*.

Ima: What causes Heaven to make harsh *gezairos* for the Jewish people?

Galia: The actions of the people cause the *gezairos*. *Tzadikim* are constantly at work for the removal of these *gezairos*.

Ima: Are you referring to the *tzadikim* in Heaven from all of the generations or the *tzadikim* that are alive in the world right now?

Galia: Both the *tzadikim* in Heaven that pray and beseech for leniency for the Jewish people and the prayers of *tzadikim* alive in the world today remove a huge number of *gezairos* that have come about because of the nation's sins. There are a lot of *tzadikim* who are ill or suffer from various unusual illnesses, and they accept this suffering lovingly to atone for the nation.

Ima: Scripture notes that when the Angel of Destruction is allowed to act, he does not distinguish between the *tzadik* and the *rasha*. In difficult times will *tzadikim* die along with the *rashaim*?

Galia: Ima, someone who is genuine and serves Hashem faithfully will not be harmed at all and it will be easier for him to get through the difficult periods awaiting us. Those who do *teshuva* and cling to Hashem have nothing to worry about at all and will not be harmed, because Hashem looks after his precious children.

Ima: But in the Holocaust, *tzadikim* died along with *rashaim*.

Galia: Ima, the Holocaust was a hard *gezaira* for the Jewish people. It was a type of *gezaira* which was impossible to remove.

Ima: Galia, you say the *geula* is very soon. How soon is soon?

Galia: I cannot say. I am just allowed to say that it's near. Ima, we are in very difficult times. The whole nation has to do *teshuva*. I cry because I am sad over what will take place in the near future. But you have to pray, read *Tehilim* and glorify and praise the One who made everything. Everything is subject to Him and the power of all functions in this world comes from the letters of His Name.

The signs show that Hashem pities us and wants to redeem us quickly. It's just that we have to increase the pace of the *teshuva* movement, and that will be wonderful for us, because the *geula* is very close. Our *geula* is already standing in the entrance and on the doorstep.

My dear mother, I want to tell you that we, this generation — are a very special generation because we are the generation of the *geula*. All the generations are jealous of us. We are lucky to have the *zechus* to live in this generation. If only we knew how to act wisely because we are capable of changing the situation. A lot depends on us and we can hasten our *geula* through a complete *teshuva* of the masses.

Ima: What do we have to do to step up the pace of bringing about the *geula*?

Galia: Ima, the pace of the *geula* will increase as the flow of people doing *teshuva* increases. The whole secret is to pray a lot, read *Tehilim*, to offer prayers to Hashem to have mercy on his people, Israel, and to lead them to the *geula* with great mercy. To stir others to return to their Father in Heaven, to work on their *midos* and to constantly improve their service of Hashem.

❧ *Mashiach*

Ima: Is the time of the *Mashiach* coming soon?

Galia: Yes, my dear Ima, mighty and wonderful revelations await us so soon. But you have to be very wary of people who define themselves as messiahs. Soon there will be confusion. At the time of the revelation of *Mashiach*, the number of people who have risen to a high spiritual level will increase, and people will see and feel things such as there never were in all the generations. As we now draw closer to the time of the *Mashiach, geula* revelations that had previously been shown only to private individuals will be shown to the public.

Ima: Is the *Mashiach* with us yet?

Galia: *Mashiach* is here with us. He is alive and with us here and now. He is all ready and waiting to be revealed. We all have to get ready to welcome him since it depends on us to determine how and when he will reveal himself.

Ima: It doesn't seem logical to me that everyone will do *teshuva.* So what then? *Mashiach* will never come?

Galia: Ima, leave your logic out of it. *Mashiach* comes in every generation and we simply don't receive him. But soon we will have to accept him. Either we prepare ourselves or Hashem will prepare us. Only through *teshuva* will we be able to welcome him quickly and without suffering.

Ima: Galia, when the *Mashiach* is revealed, how will we know that he is the true *Mashiach*?

Galia: Ima, when the *Mashiach* is revealed, everyone will know that he is the true *Mashiach.* He will have signs which will come together with him. The signs will be very clear and his authenticity will leave no doubt in the heart of anyone that he is indeed the *Mashiach* of Israel.

Ima: Everyone hopes to see *Mashiach* in his life, and if the soul sees everything, it doesn't make a difference if the person has already died because his soul can see everything, including the *Mashiach.* Isn't that so?

Galia: What you are saying is important and correct. But being able to actually see something physically is much more special, because then a person feels his involvement in the process and has an ability to influence it. As a soul, all he can do is passively reflect on the phenomenon without any ability to influence it.

Ima: Do you know how a person can be saved from the war of Gog and Magog?

Galia: Yes. The first thing is to keep *Shabbos* properly and eat the three *Shabbos* meals. Help people, give charity and do *mitzvos*, study Torah and spread Torah. Ima, very soon, the whole picture will change and things will start to be very disturbing in the world. The whole world will be like a big mixing bowl. There will be a lot of tension and a lot of conflict between nations and countries; and that will be the run up to the unavoidable Gog and Magog. Everything is going to change soon both materially and spiritually. Everything will be on the move: continents, people, and armies. Throughout the world, there will be mighty shocks in the run up to the expected *geula*.

Ima, to my great sorrow, we will still receive a mighty blow before Gog and Magog because, as I already said, this is a decree which we are not intelligent enough to cancel.

Ima: They say that the war of Gog and Magog will last seven years, and it hasn't even started. Will the *geula* be after the war of Gog and Magog?

Galia: Why are you so bothered about all these reckonings? You don't have to bother over them — this is all the calculations of Heaven. Everything can be changed, and everything depends only on us, on how we behave during this period. This alone will determine the pace of the *geula*.

Ima, I saw the terrible anguish you had when you arrived at the Western Wall. You got so sad over the exile of the *Shechina* and the destruction of the *Beis Hamikdash*. My dear Ima, everything will happen so quickly, soon, *b'ezras Hashem*. The whole desolate and destroyed Temple Mount, with its population of aliens and non-Jews spiritually defiling it with their abominations, will be cleansed of all its terrible *tum'ah* and of all its abominations. They will disappear as though they never existed. They will be swallowed in the ground and eternally erased. The whole Temple Mount will be cleansed and purified and will be able to get ready for the construction of the *Beis Hamikdash*, which will be built speedily in our days, Amen!

The next *Beis Hamikdash* will never be destroyed. The pain of the *Shechina* over its previous destruction is terrible. The *Shechina* has been crying and crying without stop from the moment the Temple was destroyed.

Very soon, if we have the *zechus*, the final *geula* of the Jewish people will take place. *HaKadosh Baruch Hu* Himself will fight the war for us and finally redeem us, quickly, may it be His will! There will be such exalted happiness in the higher worlds and the lower worlds. Everything will be changed and altered. Everything that was, will no longer exist. It will be as though it had never been. A new world will start, with new rules. A world of happiness, serenity, honesty, fairness, mutual love, love of one's fellow, and helpfulness — such a beautiful world. The world of the days of *Mashiach* is a world of extreme happiness. It closely resembles the happiness of the higher worlds. *Gan Eden* will be here in this world, my dear mother. Everyone will feel it, everyone who has the *zechus* to live here. Masses of the Jewish people may not have the *zechus* — *chas vechalila*. And only a tiny section of the whole, vast mankind of today will remain. Then a new, pure mankind will start to develop from this fine core such as there never was since *HaKadosh Baruch Hu* created man.

Ima, tell everyone to take advantage of this opportunity and accept the yoke of the Kingship of Heaven. Every *mitzva* saves us, especially keeping *Shabbos*, *tefillin*, avoiding promiscuity and improper thoughts, modesty and humility. When everything starts to really happen, Jerusalem will be the securest place in the whole world.

Chapter Six:
The Life of a Tzaddik –
Suffering – Death and Angels

Every family and town is judged
on the basis of the majority of
[the merits of] its members.
If the majority are tzadikim,
the judgment on them is eternal life;
and, therefore, if there is a child
of that type [i.e., retarded],
they will all be awarded eternal life
because the child is a perfect tzadik.

Hagahos Hasmak, in the name of
R' Eliyahu Baal Shem

Chapter Six

❧ Tzadikim

Ima: Galia, can anyone become a *tzadik?*

Galia: Everyone can be a *tzadik,* but it takes a lot of work on oneself to act for the sake of Heaven. It's hard, but you get the *zechus* depending on how hard you try. It just depends on the individual alone — how much he wants it and how much he does to get to it. Ima, a *tzadik* is on a very high level but if a person acts, does things and conducts himself in righteousness then he has an even higher level. The greatest *tzadik* is the one who controls his *yetzer hora* and does *teshuva.* We wage a daily war against the *yetzer hora*. There is no let-up. When a man thinks he is a *tzadik,* he is in bigger danger. Everyone has to make an effort in this world as though it's his last time here, and he cannot constantly return. He then remains eternally on the last level in this world.

We shouldn't forget that Heaven is more stringent with the souls of *tzadikim* and is very exacting with them. *Tzadikim* are judged very severely and based on their ability. A lot more is expected of *tzadikim* because they have greater ability than others.

Ima: What does it mean to have a dream about *tzadikim*?

Galia: Dreaming about *tzadikim* is a powerful sign that blessing and *shefa* will come to that person.

Ima: Is everyone in *Gan Eden* a *tzadik*?

Galia: In *Gan Eden* there are souls which are and which are not *tzadikim*. The *tzadikim* have a part in *Gan Eden* which is luxurious and glorious. Additionally, someone who has more *zechuyos* than sins can enter *Gan Eden* after a refinement process, but the pleasures he will have will be shallow in comparison to those of the *tzadikim* who went to such effort in this world.

Ima: Does your *zechus* also protect your father and brothers?

Galia: Ima, the *zechuyos* are a mighty protection for Abba and my brothers. Children who are *tzadikim* provide their parents with *zechuyos* in the next world and their *zechuyos* can protect them also in this world.

Ima: Once I dreamed about my grandmother, my mother's mother. She was so beautiful and tall, although while she was alive she was in fact simple and of small stature. I dreamed that she was dressed in beautiful pink clothes. In my dream she carried herself completely erect, tall, beautiful and radiant.

Galia: That's how your grandmother is in Heaven. She holds a very high stature because she is a perfect *tzadekes*. And the clothes she wears there fit in with the level of her importance.

Ima: What do you say about the death of the *tzadik*, Rabbi Ben-Tzion Abba Shaul *a"h* (died 5758), may his *zechus* protect us?

Galia: Dear Ima, every *tzadik* taken to the next world is a massive loss for the Jewish people. While alive, the *tzadik* is a mighty protection for everyone in his time, and the prayers of a *tzadik* are accepted and are atonement for the entire generation. When he dies, the defense is weakened, because there is no one to stand like a shield against the disasters. If it were not for the mercy of Heaven, a lot of troubles would result. We need a lot of people who perform a lot of *mitzvos* to protect our generation. In fact, there are masses doing *teshuva*, and Heaven is extremely pleased with this, but you have to carry on all the time and observe and fulfill Torah and *mitzvos* truthfully without falsehood. Heaven knows whether a man is serving Hashem with perfect faith, or not.

Ima: What do you suggest to the person who has become spiritually weak?

Galia: Everyone goes through downs in order to experience highs and it's a very natural process. You have to pray to Hashem and ask Him to help us to help ourselves and strengthen ourselves all the time. We in this world are perpetually tested with trials to our last dying day, and who is the victor? The one who succeeds in not stumbling during his life. It's a very hard assignment because the *yetzer hora* can tell you that you are perfect, but in fact he just wants to ruin you. When a person feels that he is a *tzadik* and perfect, a red light should light up inside him. He has to stop everything at once and do a cleaning job.

Ima: What about all the sins, if I had any? Have they been erased?

Galia: Ima, even if you had any sins once, they are in the process of being erased, disappearing and melting away. Over time, when you accept the yoke of Heaven, with Heaven's mercy, the sins turn into *zechuyos*. But I say to you again, it takes a lot of work on yourself.

❧ Pain and Suffering

Ima: What can a person do so there won't be suffering?

Galia: Ima, what Hashem wants — that's what happens. It is impossible to change everything. There are some things which Heaven has arranged for everyone.

Ima: What is the purpose of suffering in life?

Galia: Suffering is love. Hashem is trying to save us and we are a stiff-necked people. Suffering is the education process of a loving father. The goal of suffering is to bring man to the truth. You, Ima, would not have gotten there without suffering.

Ima: True. Very true. Why did you cry on *Shabbos*? Is it not correct that it is forbidden to cry on *Shabbos*?

Galia: I want to tell you that my stomach hurt me on *Shabbos*. But I am also agitated because now it's a very dangerous time for the whole world and especially for the Jews. It causes me to have stomachaches and heartache. It's true that it's forbidden to cry on *Shabbos*, but that's not a law in which I am obligated as I am mentally incompetent and as such, I am not obliged to observe *mitzvos*.

Ima: In any case, you are not capable of committing any sin.

Galia: Right, but I can rectify my past through my present condition. The situation itself brings rectification. The suffering is like fire — it purifies the soul. Ima, I know that I am due to go through more suffering. But everything is for our good. Because I will get to Heaven purified and they won't have to refine me further there in *Gehinom*. It's better to accept all the suffering here with love. Suffering purifies. In the end, what Hashem wants is what will happen. Ima, it's not possible to change everything. There are some things that we have to accept.

Ima: How is it that you accept your suffering with such great serenity and are so reconciled to all your limitations, your dependence on others, and your terrible condition? What a poor thing you are to have to suffer like this all your life. Aren't you fed up?

Galia: Ima, I accept everything lovingly because I know it's meant to consummate the soul and everything is for the good. Even if a man suffers, it's all for his good so that he can bring his soul to perfection, otherwise it would remain lacking in Heaven.

Ima: Galia, it tears me apart that you are so weak and thin and look so awful. I really suffer. I pray that you won't suffer.

Galia: Ima, that's my *tikun*.

Ima: What else were you sent to rectify in this world apart from the sin of child-rearing?

Galia: Ima, I was sent here to scrape off the dust which stuck to my soul because of the sin of child-rearing, and it's getting cleaner and cleaner and there's not much left to scrape. Ima, my suffering scrapes it clean.

Ima: What will happen when you finish the cleansing of your soul?

Galia: That is controlled by Heaven alone and it will be decided in Heaven.

Ima: You have been sent by Heaven to get me to do *teshuva*. How were you prepared to suffer so much, all this life here, instead of suffering a tiny bit in *Gehinom* and immediately going into *Gan Eden*?

Galia: My dear Ima, I was happy to come and help you, because I knew that only I could bring you to do *teshuva*. All the suffering, which is my lot in this world, is sweeter than honey and I accept it lovingly. We are all happy and glad to do the will of our Father in Heaven. What is this suffering in contrast with fulfilling the roles that Hashem has assigned to us in this world?

Ima: Why did you have spasms and contractions yesterday and pass out? I worried about you a lot and I really took it hard.

Galia: My dear Ima, I want to tell you that all these bouts of suffering have a great polishing and purifying effect. They're hard and unpleasant, but they help to cleanse and are very purifying.

Ima, it's very hard for me to be dependent on the kindnesses of others. That's the hardest thing for me in this world, but my soul sees and knows the purpose of this terrible suffering and that comforts me.

Ima: Galia, before the soul comes down to this world, do they tell it in the high world how much suffering it has to go through in its life here? Then during its life, does it suffer a little each time until it completes the quota of suffering? Or is it simply that a person's own conduct determines how much suffering he will get and when?

Galia: Ima, a person's conduct also has an influence, but all which happens to him in this world is predetermined in Heaven. A man has a pre-set plan. But every man has the possibility of changing his plan in accordance with his ma'asim tovim in this world. There are examples of people whose plan changes and they become *tzadikim* and go up a spiritual level. Everything depends on the person himself.

ᴥ *Death*

Ima: What do you say about old age and old people who are helpless and indigent?

Galia: Ima, old age is part of the *tikun* of the soul — but it's also easier for a person who gets to old age to part from this world of falsity. It's hard for people to cope with this loss.

Ima: Is dying painful? Is it frightening?

Galia: It depends for whom.

Ima: For an honest person who observes *mitzvos*.

Galia: It depends on how far he is tied to this world. It will be very difficult for somebody who really loves the pleasures of this world of falsity to leave it.

Ima: Does a man know to what age he will live?

Galia: No. Nobody knows, apart from some very exceptional people.

Ima: They say the soul knows thirty days before death that it's going to die.

Galia: Yes. But the mind of a person does not know.

Ima: When you die, do you meet up with relatives who have passed away? After one hundred and twenty years, will I meet up with my mother, *zichrona levracha*?

Galia: On entry, they'll come to greet you.

Ima: Do the relatives of all men who die come to meet the new arrival in Heaven?

Galia: Yes. That way the soul is not afraid. Hashem in His kindness arranges it so that the soul will not be afraid after death. The soul is afraid because it was so linked to the body and then suddenly, it's not.

Ima: How can a man prepare himself for dying so that his death will be easier? I have heard that a certain book describes how a person can prepare himself during his entire life for the day of his death.

Galia: Ima, everyone has to prepare himself for death because death doesn't skip over anyone. The main thing is to fulfill Hashem's *mitzvos*. It's also important not to get tied to material things, because then it is hard for a person to give up on his physical attachments which only serve to increase the sufferings of the soul.

Ima: Does the soul see everyone after its body is buried?

Galia: Ima, it sees them but it cannot say anything. It is not allowed to communicate with the living. But it suffers a great deal from the parting. In addition, if those it loved go through torment and suffering, then it also feels anguish over them in Heaven. Souls of relatives who love each other continue to be linked after death too.

Ima: Galia, they say that when a person dies, the soul mourns over the body, which has rotted. Do handicapped people with deformed bodies also mourn over their bodies after death?

Galia: Ima, they mourn less than those who have a fine body. But old people mourn even less because their bodies have stopped functioning as they should, and they are weak, and the strength to live is gone. For them it's easy to die. For those who have fine bodies and they still have their strength, it's difficult after death. Their souls really suffer.

Ima: Galia, how do you overcome the fear of death?

Galia: Ima, if a person prepares himself for death all his life, he is not afraid of dying. Because he knows that death is merely an extension of this life and that what is to come is much better.

Ima: Galia, what should you do if you yearn for someone who has died?

Galia: Ima, you separate only for a while, then you meet up again in Heaven. Until you meet, it's hard because you yearn to be with the person, and this is also part of the soul's *tikun*.

Ima: Galia, what's the thing that gives the most satisfaction to the soul after its departure from the body after death?

Galia: Ima, the *mitzvos* and *ma'asim tovim* that the person did. That's what gives him his satisfaction in Heaven and nothing else.

Ima: Why, when a man is buried, is it important to put up a tombstone over the grave? What does it do?

Galia: Ima, a man's grave is like his body's home. The body lies in the dust until the resurrection of the dead, and the body is also given compensation and pleasure for having suffered so much in its life.

❧ *Mitzvos As The Clothes Of The Soul*

Ima: What is the meaning of a man having *zechuyos*? Is it like having a reserve in the bank that he can use as he wants, when he wants?

Galia: Ima, *zechuyos* provide a person with additional credits in Heaven, and this enables him to do and receive things which people without *zechuyos* cannot. Those who have accumulated *zechuyos* here in this world from observing *mitzvos* and helping other people are provided with additional credits in the next world.

Ima: Does life really have such a power to influence and change things?

Galia: Ima, that's why it is so important for a man to fulfill *mitzvos* in this world — because that way he can bring salvation and redemption to his soul and the soul of the Jewish people. It's a great *zechus* to reach the truth and that's the purpose of this world — to see the truth amid all this concealment. To choose to follow the path of truth and fulfillment of *mitzvos,* which we have been sent here to fulfill.

Ima: They say that when a person dies, you have to hurry to bury him. What's the reason for rushing so much?

Galia: Ima, as long as the body is not buried, the soul suffers and suffers because it is not protected by the supernal clothes they dress it in after the burial. The soul suffers a lot of pain on seeing the body which has still not returned to the dust from whence it came. Also, it is judged after the burial and not before, so it's extremely important. If the person committed a lot of serious sins, the soul suffers a lot until its burial because it doesn't know what its fate will be. It finds its peace and its place only after the trial.

Ima: What do you suggest I do to ease the pain of death after I am one hundred and twenty years old?

Galia: Ima, if a person fulfills the *mitzvos* in this world, his death is not hard for him because he is happy and has pleasure from the prospect of what is waiting for him in the next world. The hardest thing is when a man gets to the next world naked of *mitzvos*. In the next world, everything is apparent. Just as in this world one can see when a man has no clothes, so too in the next world all know that he is naked of *mitzvos*. Spreading Torah is what sews the most beautiful clothing for him. They are so beautiful, that in this world you can't possibly even imagine their beauty. There, everyone is dressed according to his actions in this world.

Ima: Galia, in Heaven, does the soul get another body or does it stay without a body? Are you allowed to say?

Galia: Ima, there is no such as being without a body. Every world has the body meant for that world and its purpose. My dear Ima, in the next world which is a spiritual world, there are spiritual clothes and everything is in accordance with the person's actions and *tikun* in this world. So it is very important to perform *mitzvos* and *ma'asim tovim*, because every *mitzva* builds spiritual clothes of glory for us and adorns them with decorations beyond imagination.

Ima: Can the *mitzvos* I do add to the *zechuyos* of my mother who is in Heaven?

Galia: Ima, that's subject to change all the time. Every *mitzva* that a person does in this world goes to the credit of the parents who gave birth to him. Everyone who is part of his soul gets his *zechuyos*.

✢ Angels

Ima: They say that an angel teaches the soul of the baby in the womb the entire Torah. Does the angel teach a baby girl like a baby boy?

Galia: The whole Torah — both a baby boy as well as a baby girl.

Ima: When they say the angel teaches the baby "the Torah," do they mean the Five Books of Moses?

Galia: There is only one Torah! The angel teaches the whole Torah, including the Prophets, the Writings, *Torah she-baal peh* — the Oral Law, everything.

Ima: Do you see angels even when you are awake and not only in a dream?

Galia: Ima, that's correct.

Ima: Galia, you know there's a story on a tape by a known rabbi about a boy who died a clinical death and came back to life. While he was in a state of clinical death, he saw tens of thousands of black angels, angels of destruction and angels of bright light going up and down in this world. He saw that there is movement here all the time.

Galia: That's right. There are angels constantly coming here on some mission and the souls see it all.

Ima: Are the *mitzvos* a person does here his advocates? And if so, where are they?

Galia: Ima, they accompany him all the time and do not leave him. His advocates constantly hover around him and cut a path for him through all the troubles and terrible suffering which he might have to suffer. They fight and drive off evil and give his soul a good feeling and hover around him in the form of pure, high angels. *Mitzvos* have the power to create high spiritual powers, which accompany us forever. If a man sins, his sins create evil angels, demons, and destructive spirits which surround him and cause him difficulties in earning a living, getting married, his domestic harmony and whatever he sets about doing.

Ima: Galia, maybe you can explain to me how *mitzvos*, whose execution is in the material world, create a spiritual angel? It's hard to grasp.

Galia: It's hard to grasp a lot of things, but all the worlds are interlinked. The other worlds are spiritual and are linked to the material worlds. Spiritual actions have an effect on physical actions and physical actions have an effect on spiritual actions. It's like an AC-DC converter, it is all a perfectly integrated network of influences from world to world.

Ima: How do you know what an AC-DC converter is?

Galia: You are forgetting that if Heaven permits, I know everything. The way I look and the fact that I don't actually speak with my mouth like everyone misleads you.

Ima: Are you allowed to tell me what you see around you?

Galia: Ima, I see a lot of advocate angels around me all the time, pleading for me, *baruch Hashem*. There are literally units upon units of angels which don't let anything harmful get near me.

Ima: Is it true that every *mitzva* creates a good angel and every sin creates a bad angel?

Galia: That's correct. When the soul stands in the court in Heaven, Heaven's calculations are clear to it. The soul on trial understands and accepts his sentence. The Court of Heaven shows a man all of his deeds. They show him every word he said, every thought he thought. If he does not observe *mitzvos*, difficulties and troubles come to him like a chain, one after the other, so that he will wake up and do *teshuva* and *ma'asim tovim*. When a person sins, he creates a prosecuting angel who is allowed to harrass the sinner with all kinds of trouble and suffering.

Ima: Does one's advocate angels actually accompany a person on his journey into the next world?

Galia: Absolutely. *Mitzvos* turn into *melitzei yosher* — advocate angels. Every word and every good deed produces an angel who guards a person, and the entire Jewish people, that subsequently accompany him on his journey to the next world. The more a person accumulates *zechuyos*, the more protection there is for the person and for the nation as a whole. With sins, it's the exact opposite. Every sin creates an angel of destruction that causes both the doer, and the Jewish nation, great troubles.

Ima: Is it to be understood from what you said that the evil angels want to harm the doer?

Galia: Yes, Ima. A man's misdeeds create bad angels that are always on the lookout trying to see how they can harm him. Sins destroy at will, as far as their strength and the evil by which they were created them allow them to.

Ima: Are the good angels with a person all the time, even after he dies?

Galia: Ima, every *mitzva* creates an angel to plead for the person. When he is alive, the good angels help the person and protect him from all evil; this is certainly so in the next world, which is a spiritual world. There the soul can also *see* the angels and communicate with them.

Chapter Seven:
On Prayer and Chesed;
On Midos and Marriage

A person should not ask the tzadik
himself to answer his prayers.
A person must entreat HaKadosh
Baruch Hu, who can do everything,
to have mercy, to answer the prayer
in the zechus of the particular tzadik.
A person may ask the tzadik to plead
on our behalf, to pray for us and
ask for Heaven to have mercy on us
and on all of the Jewish people.

Galia

Chapter Seven

❧ Prayer

Ima: What power does prayer have?

Galia: Prayer has very great power. Prayer can change a person's fate. Sometimes prayer can save a person from death. Prayer can change *gezairos.*

Ima: Do you mean a person's silent prayer or does he have to pray aloud? And are you talking about the prayers in the *siddur* or in the *Tehillim*?

Galia: Prayer from the heart. Ima, you have to pray every day because it's important. Ask Hashem to send us His salvation quickly and cancel the adverse *gezairos* that are on us.

Ima: Do you pray too?

Galia: Me? Yes. Yes, all the time. It is very important not to miss out on any day's prayer.

Ima: Galia, you said you pray to Hashem. Do souls also pray?

Galia: Ima, souls also pray to Hashem and not only with the mind. You also pray with your soul and not only with your mind.

Ima: What's the meaning of a "servant of G-d"? Does it refer to a person who prays to Hashem?

Galia: Ima, a "servant of G-d" is anyone who does everything for the sake of Heaven and fulfills *mitzvos* and prays to Hashem with all his heart.

Ima: What's the meaning of "for the sake of Heaven," can you explain to me what that means?

Galia: Ima, that's when a man ignores his own desires and nullifies himself for the sake of Hashem and does things only for the sake of Heaven. In Heaven, this is regarded as a great virtue.

Ima: How important is a person's prayer? How much does it help?

Galia: Praying helps a lot. It helps a lot when *tzadikim* pray and beg Hashem to help His people and direct them on the right path. Each prayer has a very significant influence. Prayer splits the Heavens and appears before the Throne of Glory. Hashem hears every prayer and gives great preference to the prayers of His *tzadikim*. Ima, I constantly pray for my beloved Jewish people.

Ima: What should you pray with children, aside from the daily prayers?

Galia: All prayers said with children are very welcome in Heaven. They split Heavens and reach and appear before the Throne of Glory. The prayers of innocent children have such a mighty force that it's very important that they pray for the Jewish people.

Ima: How can I persuade women to pray?

Galia: Ima, the method of persuasion has to appeal to their inner being. Everything must be done pleasantly and politely. You can't force or pressure. Prayer which comes from compulsion or pressure is not prayer. It's better that they understand what they pray and whom they serve. Over time, they will enjoy the *shefa* from Heaven and go up spiritually.

Ima: What do we have to do to change the judgment so that there will not, *chas vechalila,* be a hard time for the Jews?

Galia: Ima, you have to get women together for Torah classes and *Tehillim* groups and do this all the time. This will greatly help to prevent hardships. If, G-d forbid, something bad happens, reading *Tehillim* helps a great deal and arouses Heaven's mercy. Pray a lot. Prayer has the power to change fate.

Ima: What should I concentrate on to succeed in the fulfillment of my purpose in this world?

Galia: Ima, you can give more care to your prayers because prayer has the fantastic power to bring a person closer to the Creator. It's the formula for succeeding in fulfilling one's mission in this world. Obviously, one also needs to be careful in his service of Hashem and his observance of Torah.

Ima: Somebody asked about why his prayers have ups and downs from time to time.

Galia: He has to understand that there is no one, even if he is a very holy man and great believer, who doesn't have ups and downs. Even those with very high spirituality have downs, because Heaven tests them. Or it can be a down which will be immediately followed by an up, and Heaven will open the gates of Torah study and acceptance of his prayers.

You have to know that all of life is helter skelter, and goes up and down. Sometimes you go down a little and sometimes you go up a little. It's important that the downs be small. Because all these downs are only in order to go up higher afterwards. It's like starting in a running race. You have to make a backward movement to dart forward. The main thing is not to get depressed.

Ima: Galia, why does a person have to pray if Hashem knows everything that we need and can give us everything without us asking, based on our *zechuyos*.

Galia: Ima, you asked a good question. Hashem constantly gives us massive amounts of *shefa*. If we were to open up our eyes to see just a fraction of this *shefa*, we would spend the whole day just thanking, glorifying, and praising the King of Kings, *HaKadosh Baruch Hu*, maker of everything.

My dear mother, prayer has many purposes. The most important of them is to rise to higher spiritual levels, enabling a spiritual conduit for *shefa* to come down to this world. Prayer is like a connecting pipe from this world to the high world and from the high world to this world. Prayer bridges the two worlds and allows a person to get close to the King of the World, to cling to Him, *Yisbarach*, and to rise to higher and higher spiritual levels. The *tzadik* prays for the Jewish people and brings down *shefa* to the Jews, to the entire world, and to the *tzadik* personally. The *kedusha* passes through him directly, without interference and failures. So it is extremely important to pray with great sincerity, with clean thoughts, to keep our thoughts with us and not allow them to escape and waft far away to forbidden regions.

It is very important to prepare before praying and concentrate very hard on it. Also, talking during the service and stopping the divine *shefa* from coming down to this world is very serious. Meaningful prayer in purity and holiness with great inspiration is one of the hardest assignments given the Jew in this world; and those who succeed in rising spiritually in their prayer feel an incomparable celestial happiness. They feel close to *Hashem Yisbarach*, King of the World, as though they are standing in His chamber and talking to Him directly. He, *Yisbarach,* hears us directly. True spiritual inspiration in prayer is one of the greatest pleasures a man can have and one of the important jobs a Jew has in this world. Through that he can join together higher and lower worlds.

Ima, most people don't achieve high levels in prayer. Most people pray routinely and recite their prayers without thinking of the meaning of what's written. There are always a few *tzadikim* who are always very close to *HaKadosh Baruch Hu* in their prayers. The prayers of *tzadikim* go up more easily and quickly rise to the high chambers that they are worthy of entering.

The more a man works on his *midos* and fulfills the *mitzvos* of *Hashem Yisbarach*, the more he becomes a clean and purified pipe through which the fresh water can flow very easily, in a fast, strong current, without hindrances. When the spiritual pipe is clogged with the products of sinning, it causes blockage, and sometimes the passageways are blocked beyond repair. Everything depends on the person himself, how fast his prayers get to the One Who Dwells On High, if they get to Him at all. Man is the key to change fortune. He holds the key to open his personal world and the world around him to unlimited happiness. But sometimes a man loses the key to himself and stays locked and closed.

✿ *Tehillim*

Ima: What power does saying *Tehillim* have?

Galia: A fantastic power. It arouses the mercy of Heaven on those saying *Tehillim* and the whole of the Jewish people. *Tehillim* has a fantastic power to drive off the *mazikim* — the damaging spirits from a person, and open up the gates of Heaven to extract mercy and favor. *Tehillim* erases a great deal of one's sins, and of Heaven's judgments against him. *Tehillim* also has a proven power to calm the soul.

Each and every word in *Tehillim* has a meaning whose power and ability to protect us cannot be imagined. Everything is in *Tehillim*. It is written with the highest holy inspiration (*ruach hakodesh*). King David, *alav hashalom* thought of every Jew and of every single soul. The *Tehillim* has an answer for everyone who reads it.

In reading *Tehillim*, you open up Heaven's pipelines for *shefa*, livelihood, peace, and every issue and request. Fortunate are those who read *Tehillim*. In the *zechus* of reading *Tehillim*, you can ask for a pleasant marriage partner, blessing and success.

A person who reads *Tehillim* can change their world for the better. Women in particular, have special *zechuyos*. They have unconditional belief and know how to love, and know how to feel the love of Hashem for the Jewish people. This is very pleasant to Hashem. Women have the ability to draw close to Hashem without studying Torah like men. Everyone must observe the Torah and *mitzvos*, but women are more successful in getting close to Hashem.

Ima, all the *Tehillim* said for the sick helps a great deal. It helps a man in the hour of danger. *Tehillim* has a mighty healing power. King David put into *Tehillim* powers of salvation and cure. All who read *Tehillim* with great sincerity are answered. *Tehillim* helps all the sick and the whole of the Jewish people whatever their situation, in whatever plight they are in, and the more you read, the better.

If children read *Tehillim*, then each and every request of theirs has a mighty power, because children are still simple and not corrupted by the inanities of this world.

Ima, read *Tehillim* everyday. It helps tremendously in drawing near to Hashem

ᵡᴧ *Power Of Ta'anis Dibbur*

Ima: What's the power of a *ta'anis dibbur* (a day on which one accepts upon himself not to speak)?

Galia: A *ta'anis dibbur* has a mighty influence both spiritually and materially. On the day that a person commits himself not to say a word whatsoever and read the entire book of *Tehillim* three times without interrupting to speak of worldly matters, all the rulings against him and the Jewish people are eased.

Ima, if you could see what reading the book of *Tehillim* does in Heaven, you'd drop everything and spend the whole day just reading *Tehillim*. How many lights *Tehillim* lights up! With the limited grasp you have at the moment, Ima, you cannot picture it. It's a like a big village not connected to electricity, in darkness. Every time you read *Tehillim*, every word you read, another lamp lights up; house after house lights up with an exquisite light, one after the other.

ᵡᴧ *Song Of Songs*

Ima: What is the power of saying *Song of Songs*?

Galia: *Shir Hashirim* has a fantastic power to cancel

gezairos on the Jewish people because it contains a description of how much Hashem loves us. Saying *Shir Hashirim* — even day after day — helps a great deal. It is full of higher secrets of which the average person is not at all aware. It has the power to bring much *kedusha* and *shefa* from the high worlds down to this world.

❧ Shema (at night)

Ima: What is the power of reading the *Shema* before falling asleep?

Galia: Reading the *Shema* before going sleep has a fantastic power to cancel Heaven's adverse *gezairos*. Reading the *Shema* guards all of a person's limbs from all evil and all trouble.

Dear Ima, I am happy that you read the *Shema* for me and the children in the center before we fall asleep. Your washing my hands for me as the *halacha* specifies also really helps me.

❧ The Power Of A Bracha

Galia: Every *bracha* has power. A *bracha* brings down spiritual *shefa* from the high worlds, and the greater a man's *zechuyos*, the more he succeeds in bringing down *shefa*. If the person being blessed is worthy of *shefa*, he will receive it all. Sometimes when the one blessed is unworthy of the blessing he receives, negative forces may be stirred up against him because he is unworthy of the spiritual *shefa* that heaven is giving to him.

❧ Saying Amen

Galia: The Amen which people answer to *brachos* and the *kaddish* have an extremely great virtue. It is a confirmation by us that we believe in Hashem, that he is the King of the

World, and He is the one who designed and created every single thing. He is the one and only Ruler, the source of all powers, unlimitedly powerful and ruling over all the worlds. In saying Amen, we lovingly confirm this. Our Amen also confirms and indicates the extent of our love for our Creator and the Creator of all the worlds. In answering Amen, we actually ask Hashem, the King of the World, to give us of His good and send down great *shefa* to His beloved Jewish people.

❧ *Spreading Torah*

Galia: Spreading Torah stands like a mighty rock. He who spreads Torah is helped by Heaven in everything. Today, people are so desperately in need of every crumb of *kedusha,* teaching them Torah is like saving them in the middle of the desert and giving them water so they don't wither.

Ima, in Heaven they are pleased with all of the efforts that exist to spread Torah to the masses. We are in a time which is extremely important for us and the *geula* is really close. The hard work of those who disseminate Torah actually saves masses of people from going to their destruction. My dear mother, carry on with all your strength because it's really a matter of actually saving lives. Strengthening people today is their salvation. There is great joy in Heaven from the great religious revival of the Jewish people. If only they will continue like this with all their might. It really helps the Jewish people that there are people for whom it is so imperative to spread Torah.

Ima: Galia, I read that there is a special gate in *Gan Eden* that only those who are *mezakeh es harabim* — give the masses *zechus* — can enter. What do say about that?

Galia: Ima, it's correct that in Heaven there are special privileges for people who are *mezakeh harabim*. They work so hard in our closed world, which is just beginning to be opened up, and absorb the fact that the world has a king and He is *HaKadosh Baruch Hu*, and that there is no one besides Him. All the autistic children like me who convey the word of the living G-d, all come from Heaven to help us see that Hashem is the King of the World. He is One and the One and Only King, the Supreme Power beyond all challenge; He has absolute control of the whole creation and the universes, and there is no one besides Him. His power and wisdom fill the world. There is no limit and there is no means of measuring the extent of His exclusive power over all the worlds.

Hashem gives a lot of powers to anyone who wants and tries to spread Torah. Even if it seems to a person that he has no abilities, Heaven will send him mighty powers, and he won't even know from where they are coming. His reward will be very great in Heaven. Spreading Torah is one of the most important *mitzvos* in this world. They should continue with all their strength and to the limits of their power.

Ima: Galia, how can I make you happy and provide you joy in this material life, in addition to visits and communicating?

Galia: Ima, nothing in particular. Only your *mitzvos* and your *ma'asim tovim* and your spreading Torah can make me happy in this world of falsity.

Ima: Do you have any advice about how we can be saved from *Gehinom*?

Galia: You can be saved from *Gehinom* through spreading Torah. A man is not obligated to spread Torah in our world. Heaven treats the person who spreads Torah with great kindness. He is thought of as one who is kind to others for the sake of Heaven. Spreading Torah is one of the proven formulae for being saved from *Gehinom*.

The path of spreading Torah leads to high levels and every elevated effort a person puts into bringing sons and daughters back to their Father in Heaven is regarded as a an act of great virtue. Heaven will reward us for what we do for His name out of love. Any act of spreading Torah by any Jew arouses great happiness in Heaven. Anyone who spreads Torah is put in the category of those who bring the *geula* closer. We are near the end. *Mashiach* will arrive and be revealed to the Jewish people awaiting him impatiently, *b'ezras Hashem*. Heaven guides the disseminators of Torah and helps them inspire the listeners to walk on the path of Torah and the *mitzvos* of *Hashem Yisbarach*. They help someone who has the *zechus* to talk and hold the interest of the audience with what he says. It seems to us that **we** prepare what to say, but *HaKadosh Baruch Hu* actually puts the words in our mouths. Our prayer has to be: *May the words which we shall have the zechus to be placed in our mouths strengthen the audience for Heaven's sake.*

Any act of spreading Torah in Israel is like air for breathing, to bring the *geula* closer in these difficult days – the days of the redemption of the Jewish people. Ima, don't be afraid of anything. Hashem protects all those who go out and spread Torah, who do it for His name, to fetch in His lost children. Disseminators of Torah get a lot of Heavenly help. *HaKadosh Baruch Hu* loves those who bring his children to their Father in Heaven.

✤ *The Power of Speech*

Ima: I learned about speaking badly of people — *loshon hora* — and the power of speech. Speech has a fantastic power. I didn't realize it.

Galia: Speech does have a fantastic power. It's actually a flaming stonecutter — both for the better and for the worse. Every word a man says is extremely important. Words have a strong influence and you have to be careful. You have to be aware of the importance in Heaven of every single word, and be very careful, because words have an amazing ability to build and to destroy.

Ima: I learned that every word you say is so important and influential that you have to be extremely careful not to say *anything* bad. You have to be so careful with your words that maybe it's a good idea not to speak at all.

Galia: Ima, it's a good idea to talk as little as possible, only as much as you have to, and no more.

Ima: Is speaking badly of someone such a serious sin that people come back to the world in a *gilgul* because of the sin of speaking badly about others? I communicated with a young man with autism and he replied that he is a great *tzadik* who came to the world to make good on the sin of speaking badly. Can you be sent back just because of the sin of speaking badly?

Galia: Ima, it's a very serious sin and you certainly can be sent back to this world for it. Speaking badly of people is one of the worst sins a man can commit, because he brings accusations on others as well as on himself.

Ima: Can you say something about oaths?

Galia: You have to understand that the power of words is vast and great. Words build in the high worlds and destroy in the high worlds. Here, too, words have the power of destruction and ruin, and building and life. You pay a high price in all the worlds for false oaths. Tell everyone to be careful about swearing and cursing. They have a mighty survival power and a grave and serious damaging effect. A person should completely refrain from swearing and cursing. A person should teach and condition himself to speak purely and without swearing.

৯৬ *Charity*

Ima: Can you talk about charity?

Galia: Ima, charity is a very great virtue. It's a *mitzva* that can save a person from death. It's a very great *mitzva* and gives a person special *zechuyos* in Heaven. Charity is kindness and always a wonderful thing to do for anyone at any time. It helps a great deal to donate with a loving heart and true desire to help unfortunate people and those who suffer, and make their hardship easier. The charity a man gives accompanies him to Heaven and provides powerful protection both in this world and the afterworld. The individual contributions are like angels who go along with the person and guard him all the time.

Ima, the world exists because people help each other. If people did not help each other, the whole world would not be able to survive for even a moment. The world would return to emptiness and void. All the kindnesses which we do here hold up the foundations of the high worlds. Kindness is the basis of our survival.

Without helping others, we would not survive. Those who help others are in fact helping themselves and ensuring the continuation of their existence and others'. If no one in the world would help anyone, no one would survive. And if people do help others, the world and everyone will continue to survive.

Ima: Can you tell me something about *ma'aser* (donating one tenth to charity)?

Galia: Ima, *ma'aser* is a *mitzva* of the Torah. We are commanded to give a tenth of our income to charity and the donations we make help us more than we help others. Our helping others and giving charity create angels who plea on our behalf in this world and the next world.

✿ Anger

Ima: Why is anger considered to be the worst *mida*?

Galia: Ima, someone who gets angry and doesn't control himself is thought of as an idolator. Anger is at the root of so many sicknesses of the body and the soul. People who get angry must work on themselves as soon as possible because getting angry even once can ruin all of the work of months in which they performed a tremendous amount of *mitzvos*. Getting angry just once erases large volumes of the blessings which the person was supposed to receive. Ima, tell everyone that the source of anger is the *sitra achra* whose whole object is to confuse us and distance us from Torah and *mitzvos*. This is one of our hardest tests in this world. You have to make the effort not to get drawn to the *yetzer hora* which tells us to get angry.

We are commanded to work on this trait, as on other traits, bit by bit. The most important thing to do when you get angry is simply to keep quiet. When your anger strikes, you talk and think differently. When you're angry, you can say some very serious things beyond your control because the *sitra achra* helps you to say things for which sometimes you cannot apologize, and there's no means of atoning for them.

✿ Love

Ima: What can you tell me about love?

Galia: Love is the feeling of never being alone. It is the need to feel that somebody cares about you. Love of this kind is a refuge from the hard world. Love has to be for the sake of Heaven, based on the laws of the Torah. G-d's love is an example to us, because Hashem loves us unconditionally. Even if we rebel and go far from Him, He still loves us, His children. Hashem loves all of us, like a mother who loves of all of her many children. Love without conditions and for the sake of Heaven is true love.

When a man and a wife love each other, it has to be a holy thing and without physical conditions. He and she, together with Hashem, build a small *Beis Hamikdash*, and it's all for the sake of Heaven. The greatest love in a marriage is based on the fact that it is an opportunity to do His will. Also, in loving a child, we are doing the will of Hashem, and educating the child to serve Hashem. This is the greatest love and happiness for a father and mother to have.

In the afterworld, the limitless love and *shefa* of Hashem will be toward all of His creatures. Those who have toiled all their lives in this world in Torah, *mitzvos* and *ma'asim tovim* will be the ones to feel his love in the greatest measure.

All love comes directly from Hashem. Hashem is all love. In the afterworld, there is the limitless love of *HaKadosh Baruch Hu* for all His creatures and there is a limitless·*shefa* of a love beyond human understanding. It belongs only to the person who has the *zechus* to receive this limitless happiness.

Ima: Why is it so important for you to be at home with me on *Shabbos*?

Galia: Ima, being close to you causes me great happiness. Only you give me true love and that is what keeps me going. Your love gives me the strength to continue. I feel that I am not alone in this world of falsity. Without love, you feel alone here in this world. Your love, your hugs and kisses, give me the strength to carry on living.

My dear Ima, I love you very much. You cannot even imagine how attached we are to each other. It's very hard for a person to live without love. A man cannot live without love. He is not built to live his life without the love of someone in the world. A man's greatest life force is the love he can give and receive.

Ima: Galia, I love you very much. A lot of women and girls who hear my talks about you tell me to tell you that they love you. They send you kisses and bless you with a full recovery. Does that help you?

Galia: I get happiness from all the women who send me true love. I feel their love helping me and giving me more strength to continue here in this world which is so full of pain and suffering.

✤ *Honesty*

Ima: What can you do so that there will be more honest people in the world — so that everyone will be honest?

Galia: My dear Ima, let's pray that everyone opens up his eyes to see and understand that the material aspect of life is not the main thing. Not all that is apparent to the eye is in fact true and he who relies on a person is relying on a thing empty of all content. Materialism, drives and lusts are like consuming fires that damage spirituality.

If everyone were to understand that there is One Ruler in the world from whom everything is created, and fear Him and observe the *mitzvos* of His Torah, everyone would be honest and truthful. This is the time of the *Mashiach's* coming. The soul of the Jewish race will be consummated soon. This is the true pleasure, The spiritual perfection that the soul craves all the time. It's hard for us to understand and appreciate these spiritual things with the mind.

Someone who lies will not be given eternal life. Even if he does other *mitzvos* — it doesn't help him. Because there is no possibility of him entering *Gan Eden* if he lies. In *Gan Eden*, there is no place for liars.

❧ Perfecting Your Character

Galia: We must improve our situation in every sphere of *midos*. Everything depends on each person's desires. It's hard but anyone can improve his *midos* if he wants to badly enough and works on it, and the man who works on his *midos* will reach the afterworld in a state of perfection. All your life, you have to carry on and work on your *midos* and on everything. Life is hard work and fulfilling *mitzvos* and working on *midos* is a part of the huge effort.

Ima, working on *midos* is one of our assignments in this world and it's one of the most important assignments. But if one does not perfect his *midos*, then he won't be able to blend in. It's like putting a rusty cog in a machine. If you put it in the machine, then the whole machine won't run.

❧ Marital Harmony

Galia: Marital harmony is one of the most important things that a person has in this world.

Dear Ima, the greatest case of quarrels and arguments is people not observing the laws of family purity properly. As a result, everything in the marriage becomes contaminated. The *Shechina* and peace have no ability to reside where there is *tum'ah*.

Marital harmony is one of the most important things in a person's life. If a person has a disharmonious marriage, nothing works out. Everything turns on marital harmony. If it's good in the home, the *Shechina* is in the home. Then there is ample income and blessing in every act. It projects all around a person wherever he goes and whatever he does.

Therefore, we have to treat peace in the home (*shalom bayis*) as a lofty and elevated thing and completely dedicate ourselves to it with a view to giving in and being forgiving and flexible in our views, preserving mutual trust and respecting our partners. If we work on reducing our inner pride, we will have the *zechus* of many good things, including peace, which brings with it happiness, serenity, love for each other, a good atmosphere in the home and out of it, and the *Shechina* in the home. Everything revolves around peace.

It's important to make an effort and take care of a good marriage relationship and encourage understanding between yourself and your spouse. Peace influences spiritually and materially. When husband and wife live in peace, their financial situation also improves.

Chazal *said: If man and wife do the right thing, the* Shechina *is between them. If they don't do the right thing, fire consumes them. If they do the right thing —* the name of HaKadosh Baruch Hu *is between them: the letter* **yud** *in the Hebrew word for man and the letter* **hey** *in the Hebrew word for woman join to form the word for Hashem, Y-a. If they don't do the right thing, fire consumes them — the Hebrew word for man without the letter* **yud** *spells* **aish** *meaning fire and the Hebrew word for woman without the letter* **hey** *also spells* **aish,** *meaning fire. Fire with fire.*

⤳ *Marriage And Putting Two People Together*

Ima: What's the purpose of marriage? Why do you get married?

Galia: In order to fulfill the *mitzva* of "Be fruitful and multiply" as well as that of building a Jewish home, which is like the *Beis Hamikdash.* A man has an obligation to marry. He is not allowed to be without a wife because he can commit sins.

Ima: What is the role of a woman in this world?

Galia: To be a help to her husband. Help him study Torah, create a holy life, raise children to love Hashem, and build a mini *Beis Hamikdash* in the home. If a man and his wife love each other unconditionally, for the sake of Heaven, that is true love, and it will bring success to all of their endeavors.

Ima: Is a woman who does not have a husband unable to fulfill her role in this world?

Galia: She is able to help people. Because any act of kindness that she does is like a child to which she has given birth.

Ima: Galia, when a couple gets married, are all their sins really forgiven?

Galia: Ima, Heaven erases the sins of every couple that gets married, and starts a new page. If they succeed in going on the path of Hashem, Heaven has no further reckoning with them over the past, but if they veer off the path, then their past is also taken into account.

Ima: Can you give me more information about marriage and about the pairing off of a couple?

Galia: Dear Ima, a couple put together through sorcery will quickly fall apart and won't be a successful couple. Heaven does not allow such forces to interfere with the work of *Hashem Yisbarach*. Every couple that gets together through amulets and non-Jewish charms fails in the end.

The whole issue of pairing is very deep. It involves consummation of past *gilgulim*. Sometimes a marriage ends in divorce because one partner has completed its *tikun* with the other partner. Every man gets the woman who is suited to him based on his deeds and the effect of his *gilgul*. A person should not have complaints and make accusations against Heaven. Who is suited to whom and for what reason are all the calculations of Heaven, even when the couple appears to be unsuited.

⇘ Bringing Up Children

Ima: Galia, you told me you came back to this world because of a sin in child-rearing. Is bringing up children so serious that you must suffer here for so long?

Galia: Ima, a failure in proper child rearing is as if one is killing entire generations.

Ima: What did you do wrong in the way you brought them up?

Galia: I didn't make a point of teaching them the most important things — Torah, *mitzvos* and *ma'asim tovim*.

Ima: But you said that my father *z"l*, your son in your last gilgul, entered *Gan Eden*!

Galia: Heaven is more exacting with the souls of *tzadikim* and is very demanding of them. *Tzadikim* are judged very stringently and they are judged on their capabilities. Much more is demanded of *tzadikim* because they have a much higher capability than do others.

Hashem through His great love for us teaches us, sometimes with candy, and sometimes with slaps. If we understand what He wants and learn the lessons, then the eternal life is very good.

Ima: How is it that two children from the same family who get the same education grow up to be so different from one another? One grows up to become a *tzadik*, while the second one doesn't.

Galia: Ima, one can and wishes to conquer his *yetzer hora* and the second prefers the life which he enjoys. There are conscious processes and there are subconscious ones. That's the reason why upbringing is so important.

Ima: Does the soul in Heaven after one hundred and twenty years start anew like a baby and little by little find itself?

Galia: No, Ima.

Ima: Is Heaven a continuation? Does the soul carry on from the point where it left off here?

Galia: Right. It's the next stage. Ima, bringing up children is one of the most important and toughest assignments a person has in this world. Because what he teaches and what he sows, that's what he'll reap; and that's what the world will reap too. So it's a good thing to invest a lot in bringing them up when they're young.

Tell everyone that it's in their interests to invest a great deal in bringing up children because they'll get all the *zechuyos* for doing so. If their children go on the path of Hashem, it also goes to the credit of their parents. Heaven is delighted with all the children who embark on the path of Torah. They are happy, and fortunate is their lot and the lot of their family. It's a time of favor. Heaven provides a lot of help to all those who take the first step and give their children a religious education and to all the many blessed people who assist in this holy work. Every child who transfers to receive a Torah education hastens the end of the exile and the revelation of *Mashiach tzidkainu*.

Ima: Galia, I thought about the fact that you sinned in child-upbringing and, lo and behold, in your *tikun*, you are in fact educating me and teaching me, and by doing so, you are making good [*metakeyn*] the sin in child-upbringing.

Galia: Ima, you understand things. This is in fact the *tikun* of child-upbringing. To educate is the *tikun* for education. And what you said is correct.

Chapter Eight:
Messages to Jewish Women

**The entire glory of the king's daughter
is inside the home,
greater than golden settings
is her garment.**

Tehillim 45:14

Chapter Eight

*I*ma: Do you have a message for the ladies who come to hear Torah lectures?

Galia: Ima, tell all the ladies who come to hear words of Torah that their reward is enormous and huge in Heaven. They prefer to listen to the words of Hashem over all other empty things and this is regarded as great righteousness and piety.

Women's meetings are a big *zechus* for the whole Jewish people and they get rid of large quantities of *tum'ah* and put the Jewish people in a good light and soften up all the future blows. Tell the beloved Jewish women not to get anxious or fear anything and especially not all the turmoil which the world is about to be thrown into, which is all for good and for blessing. They should put their trust in *Hashem Yisbarach* and work a lot on having trust and know that only *HaKadosh Baruch Hu* decides everything. If you have *mitzvos* and *ma'asim tovim* to your credit, then you need not fear.

Ima, tell each Jewish woman that Heaven regards her as the precious king's daughter. *HaKadosh Baruch Hu* looks upon us from Heaven and sees each precious daughter of His and is delighted and happy with her and her *ma'asim tovim* and all those ladies who try to come closer.

Dear Ima, *HaKadosh Baruch Hu* sees that there are also daughters of His, whom He loves, who do not behave and dress properly and *HaKadosh Baruch Hu* weeps over them. Hashem loves all His beloved people. Modesty is critical for us. It is one of the biggest and most serious problems of this final generation, a generation in which immodesty has spread in every direction. *HaKadosh Baruch Hu* is waiting for the whole flock to arrive, including the most distant and the slowest. Otherwise, the wolves will get them.

My dear Ima, Heaven asks every Jewish woman to be careful about being modest inside the home and out of it; and to keep the laws of family purity, which are vital for our existence. Every woman should undertake to keep *Shabbos*, to work on her character, and to be an *aishes chaiyil*. Modesty is the air we breathe. It is in our arteries and blood. The lack of it is responsible for our destruction and the shedding of our blood. It can raise us up or lower us down.

Today, modesty is a dreadful breach in our fence. Anyone who wants can get in and help himself. All the forces of evil and the *sitra achra* take advantage of the breaches and they get inside and take anything they can get their hands on. Then, all of us are judged together. Tell everyone to close up the terrible breaches that have opened up. With the power of modesty, we can drastically close and diminish all the huge holes that have opened up in the fence and the ramparts of the Jewish people, in our defense. Any woman who undertakes to be modest will close mighty gaps which have opened up. She will stop the forces of impurity that are getting at the Jewish people and causing it continuous, daily sorrows. The wish to be like non-Jews and to copy them has caused enormous sorrows to the Jewish people in all times.

✢✣ *Covering The Hair*

Galia: A Jewish woman is the king's daughter and obligated to cover her hair and there is no room here for compromise.

The modesty of the Jewish woman is like the air we breathe. Covering the hair testifies to modesty. If women knew the punishment they receive for everyone who sees their hair, they would be afraid of showing it in public.

Hair draws attention to the woman and confuses those who see her. That's why it is important that she cover her hair and every single part of the flesh of the body, so only her face and the ends of her fingers should be exposed. Everything else must be encased like a precious jewel more valuable than gold and pearls, completely closed up in a jewelry box, preserved and protected. This is true of the Jewish woman who is the jewel of the Jewish people.

If up until now she has caused the public to sin, she can do *teshuva* quickly, which in these days of good will, will be accepted with love. All of the charge sheets listing her demerits due to her lack of modesty and many sins will be deleted. All this, if she has really and truly decided to undertake modest self-presentation, including covering her body and hair according to the requirements of our law. Covering the hair is like wearing a steel helmet which protects the head during war time. That way, there is a spiritual guard against disasters and hard *gezairos*.

In regard to all the other questions as to which type of hair covering is correct, every Jewish woman must contact a rabbi and consult him about the types of covering adopted and allowed by the law in all the religious communities of Israel. And one should not deviate from what the *poskim* [religious legal authorities] say because their pronouncements are affirmed by Heaven. Otherwise they would not be chosen as *poskim* for the Jewish people.

❧ *Modesty And Fighting Immorality*

Galia: Ima, tell women that in Heaven, the woman is regarded as very precious and all her glory is inside the home. A woman is not allowed to be ostentatious or dress immodestly. Anybody looking at an immodest woman sins a great sin and Heaven will punish him and the woman who caused him to sin.

Modesty is lifesaving because a man can die because of his sins and immodesty can overload a man's sins and bring him to be judged unfavorably. Heaven will send great rewards to women who dress modestly.

Ima: What's the best way to put a stop to the immodesty in the world?

Galia: You can do it through good people and *tzadikim* who organize Torah classes and explain and teach the subject to the people. Ima, there is a lot of immodesty among our people and Hashem will not let it go on. Hashem loves us and will protect us from this plague too, but sometimes you have to educate a child with a few slaps and then he understands. Of course, it's better for him to understand without getting hit.

✤ *Family Purity*

Galia: Ima, it's important that every married woman immerse in the *mikva*. Immersion causes the purification of her soul and that she be with her husband in purity. The children born to them will come to this world in holiness, and this will give them the initial basis for searching for the truth and the path of the holy Torah.

A woman's purity enables her to bring children to the world with holy souls and these souls will have a natural desire to look for the path of Hashem. Family purity and going to the *mikva* are so important because holiness clings to holiness and impurity is drawn to impurity.

Part 3

Chapter Nine:
A New Spring In the World, Eretz Yisrael and Torah

"HaKadosh Baruch Hu said,
'I will not come to
the Heavenly Jerusalem, until
I come to the earthly Jerusalem.'"

Maseches Ta'anis

Chapter Nine

✿ *Nature — Change in Seasonal Patterns*

Ima: I dreamed of a beautiful blue sky covered from one end to the other with white storks. Do you know what that means?

Galia: Ima, that's a wonderful dream because storks tell us that spring is near and of the changes of the seasons. Very soon, there will be changes in the seasons and mighty changes and variations to all the world processes and then the spring will come — a new spring for Israel and for all of mankind.

Ima: Maybe you know. Is there a special reason for the fact that rain fell now in the month of August, in the middle of the summer? Rain never falls in the middle of the summer in Israel.

Galia: Ima, rain falls at unexpected times when those in Heaven are sad and worried over us. Because there's going to be a very difficult period very soon, and Heaven is crying over us because we'll suffer a lot from it, and it's painful, but apparently unavoidable. A major portion of the nation is in a deep slumber and has to wake up so that there will be people to receive *Mashiach* soon. Every calamity is for the benefit of the precious Jewish people.

❧ *The Rainbow*

Ima: Yesterday, on the second of *Cheshvan*, a rabbi and I saw a double rainbow in the sky. A rainbow and another rainbow above it.

Galia: You saw a double rainbow? It is something extremely rare and rare in its beauty. Such a beautiful rainbow from one end of the sky to the other end of the sky and over the whole horizon is something unusual. It indicates to us that we are entering a very unusual period in which great and mighty things will happen to my beloved Jewish people.

❧ *Hail*

Ima: Galia, what can you say about the hail that fell on *Succos*? A family from Gush Katif spoke on the radio about the storm they experienced on *Shabbos* afternoon on *Succos*. It rained, and hail came down, as big as crystal stones the size of eggs! They were frightened and said the *Shema*.

Galia: Ima, that hail is a sign from Heaven that Hashem is King of the world and He decides what will happen and to whom. Hail shows us our nothingness again and again.

❧ The Great Heat

In the summer of 1998, a massive heat wave prevailed in Israel and other areas in the world for a number of weeks. It was almost impossible to bear. There had not been a heat wave like it for many decades.

Ima: I wanted to ask you, Galia. What do you have to say about the terrible heat wave that has been going on for a number of weeks now? I have heard that people abroad have actually been dying of this heat.

Galia: My dear Ima, the heat is a sign to the Jewish people that we are existing in unusual times. Such heat is oppressive and normally does not occur with such severity. We don't have heat like this, except on rare occasions. It comes to bring a message and wake us up and ask why. If we start to inquire and ask why, we can get to the absolute truth: that Hashem is the ultimate power and that there is no force greater than Him. Only *HaKadosh Baruch Hu* can save us, not only from this heat but from all difficulties and all the difficult times.

❧ Hurricane Mitch

Ima: Galia, what do you say about the natural disaster in central America? Twenty thousand people died in Hurricane Mitch and over a million and a half people have been left without a roof over their heads (winter 1998).

Galia: Dear Ima, you understand that this is purely the hand of Hashem. The *geula* is already starting and these are signs which are starting in the whole world, bit by bit, and each time, the disasters will increase and their force will increase. This disaster is a miniature in comparison to what is awaiting the whole of mankind. Soon there will be more hurricanes and tornadoes in the States and the whole world, which will sow ruin and destruction with masses of dead and loss of property. Wind, which is something insubstantial, in a half an hour can destroy and ruin homes and material objects. And if a wind like this fulfills the commandments of Hashem, well, He can certainly do everything.

✿ *Drought*

Ima: My dear Galia, maybe you can write out for me why there is no rain? There is a real drought. We are in the height of the winter (1999); but all we've had is a tiny amount of rain.

Galia: My beloved mother, this is also one of the signs *Hashem Yisbarach* is sending us to open our eyes. If people transgress what the *Shema* demands of them, the first damage caused is drought. If we don't fulfill its commands, then immediately, "The Heavens will be closed and there will be no rain and the land won't provide produce."

The danger is very real. All these unusual things that are happening, and which will happen more all the time, are an indication to us of our unusual situation. The fact that Hashem is waiting for us to return to Him, to ask the questions *why* and *how,* to look into things and check and see that scientific responses do not give answers to many questions. If we think about it, we will see that despite man's feeling that he controls everything, man doesn't have any control. In fact, man has a complete absence of control of natural disasters or death, which he cannot deal with at all. How is it that people who think they are intelligent don't open their eyes to see and think about what's going on around them and understand that everything is from *Hashem Yisbarach*, and we don't have control of anything?

✤ *Earthquakes*

Ima: What are you allowed to say about earthquakes? What are they meant to indicate to us?

Galia: Ima, earthquakes are a sign and signal that Hashem is displeased with the actions of Man, who does not do His will. Hashem is angry with us and is indicating to us to stop our evildoing.

✤ *Eclipse of the Sun*

Ima: What is the meaning of a solar eclipse?

Galia: The eclipse of the sun is a bad omen for the world. It's a sign of imminent disasters. As I told you, this is the great quiet before the great storm. The eclipse which took place can demonstrate to us that although the sun is shining, something hid the light from reaching us. In that eclipse, it was the moon. And in the eclipse of the world, it is the forces of *tum'a,* to whom we give the ability to nurture us and hold onto us, although they are destroying everything that is good. We are near the end. As time goes on, the confusion will grow.

Whoever is still in the hands of the forces of *tum'a* will suffer a great deal, because they are *tum'a's* last link and bastion in this world, and *tum'a* will not give up on these people easily.

Therefore, get rid of all your base desires and drives, which are enticing you and driving you to the side of evil, wickedness, and *tum'a*. My dear people, get near to *Hashem Yisbarach* who gave us the Torah of truth, the

Torah of life, a present from the treasury of the King of Kings, *HaKadosh Baruch Hu*. It is the holy Torah which can raise us up from the lowest level we currently exist upon and take us up to levels of holiness and purity and join the higher spheres with the lower spheres.

❧ Helicopter Accident

Ima: What can you say about the collision of two helicopters near the northern border?

Galia: Tell everyone not to allow the news that they hear to break them. We have to continue to trust in Hashem, and know that whatever happens to us is truth. Hashem is the perfect absolute judge, and it's not within our scope to understand everything. Ima, Heaven is sad today, and so is the world.

❧ Birds

Ima: What do you say about birds who chirp a lot in the morning and evening? I have the feeling that they are simply praying to Hashem. Could that be right?

Galia: Ima, that's right. Birds, as well as all of Hashem's creatures, praise Him every evening and every morning. The fact that we don't understand their language does not mean that they do not have the ability to praise their Creator. Ima, the birds praise and glorify Hashem every morning and evening before going to sleep. We too are also commanded to give praise and thanks to Hashem daily.

❧ The Dove

Ima: Can you tell me something about the dove?

Galia: Ima, the dove is similar to the *Shechina*. It is a bird which loves and longs for its mate just as Hashem longs for us, the Jewish people. He loves us and has waited for us for so many years. We don't understand how much Hashem loves us, wants us and longs for us.

✦ *Cycles of the Year — Shabbos*

Galia: The holy *Shabbos* is the queen of the week and was given to us as a present from Hashem to gather strength and energy for the whole week. Ima, the *Shabbos* looks after the person who looks after the *Shabbos*. If a person keeps *Shabbos*, it's as though he keeps all the *mitzvos*, because *Shabbos* has a special holiness for the Jewish people, which the other days of the week do not have. The *Shabbos* is a great present to the Jewish people. A soul in Heaven suffers if its children do not keep the *Shabbos*.

Ima: Do two angels accompany a person on his way home from *shul* on Friday night?

Galia: The angels accompany the father and the son. Sources state that two angels accompany a person on his way home from *shul*, one good and one evil. The mother receives the good angel because she sees to it that the good angel stays. She prepares the home and the *Shabbos* table. The good angel stays over the whole of *Shabbos* and everything depends on the wife. If she is a good wife who has prepared for the *Shabbos*, then the angels stay in the home the whole *Shabbos,* and this brings great *kedusha* to the home.

Ima: Some of the women who came to my lecture asked me to ask you about the *melave malka,* the ritual meal held after *Shabbos* to accompany the *Shabbos* Queen upon her departure.

Galia: Ima, it's incredible to part with the Queen of the whole week (the Shabbos Queen). When you take leave of a real king and queen, you accompany them on their way out. All the servants stand at attention until they leave. So too with the departure of *Shabbos*. When the holy Queen leaves to set out on her way, we all accompany her and then wait for her to come back in a week's time.

❧ *Tu BeShevat — The 15th Of Shevat*

Ima: What can you say about *Tu Be-Shevat*?

Galia: *Tu Be-Shevat* is a wonderful time for nature. Anyone who wants to marvel at the wonders of the creation should look around and see what a beautiful world *HaKadosh Baruch Hu* made for us — a world full of colors and flowers, sun and skies. And everything harmonizes with us so beautifully in our wonderful world. We are the only ones who can decide whether it will be a beautiful world or whether it will be a world of suffering and pain. Torah and *mitzvos* are our only means of being guided on the right path. They are what will help us build a beautiful world, akin to the beautiful time in nature on the 15th of Shevat.

❧ *Purim*

Galia: Ima, my soul is extremely happy on the day of the *Purim* celebration. A great *shefa* of spiritual illumination comes down to this world today. *Baruch Hashem* that we have the massive love of the King of Kings, who chose us as His people and loves us so much. He saves us from the *rashaim* who plot our destruction in every generation. Hashem performs many mighty miracles for us all the time, and anyone who opens his eyes will see that the whole survival of the Jewish people is one big miracle. If it wasn't for that, we wouldn't be able to survive amid all the terrible hate and jealousy coming at us from all directions. In every generation, new

Haman figures stand up against us to seek our destruction and only Hashem saves us from them.

Ima: Galia, they say that the Jewish people were punished and nearly destroyed because they enjoyed participating in the feast of the wicked Achashvairosh. But I understand that the Jews ate kosher food in the feast, served in kosher dishes. So why were they punished and almost destroyed?

Galia: Ima, it is untinkable to sit down at a feast and to break bread with an avowed idolater. The Jewish people who are holy and pure must keep themselves separate from such a person.

❧ *Tisha B'Av*

Ima: Galia, do you have something to say in the time leading up to *Tisha B'Av*?

Galia: I have to say that's it's a very sad time for the Jewish people. In Heaven they cry on this day, because they long to see Israel redeemed, and we are still unworthy of it. But soon Hashem will help us and we shall be redeemed and build the Temple.

Ima: But Galia, they say that the third temple will come down from Heaven.

Galia: Ima, that's correct, but we in this world have to contribute to its material construction and Heaven will consummate it spiritually.

Ima: Last *Tisha B'Av*, I read about the destruction of the Temple and everything that happened to the Jewish people, the terrible siege, the terrible murder and slaughter, the suffering and the hunger. Suddenly, I started to get very afraid because someone who doesn't go on the path of Hashem is punished very severely.

Galia: Ima, you don't have to be afraid of *HaKadosh Baruch Hu*. No one but Him loves us without limit and watches over us endlessly. He is with us always and will never give up on us because we are His beloved nation, more than all nations and all times.

So Ima, don't worry, because the destruction came after a very long period of grave sinning in which the Jewish people transgressed the *mitzvos* of the Torah, and it was impossible to forgive them anymore. But since they are so beloved, Hashem has looked after them for thousands of years until this very day, and has not wiped them out as he has totally wiped out other nations in history.

✌ *Rosh Chodesh*

Galia: *Rosh Chodesh* is a festival day which recurs every month. On *Rosh Chodesh*, there is a massive spiritual *shefa* which comes down to the world, more than on other days. Hashem is happy with those of his sons and daughters who go His way and remember His festivals and special occasions.

Rosh Chodesh is a holy time, like a minor festival, and the special prayers provide blessing to all those who walk on Hashem's path. Tell the women that it's very important to light a candle and note this holy day which Hashem gave especially to women. It is the women, who are the main aspect of the home, who can bring about a lot of change in the home and fantastic *shefa* to their families.

✌ *Rosh Hashanah*

Galia: On *Rosh Hashanah*, everyone has to pray very seriously and with very deep and pure sincerity, and ask our Father in Heaven to pity us and remove all the hard *gezairos*. Whether or not the *gezairos* are removed depends on us.

We have to take hold of ourselves and quickly return to our Father in Heaven. *Rosh Hashanah* is a test for the Jewish people. Hashem in His mercy gives us another chance and we have to know how to take advantage of this for the good, for a blessing and do complete *teshuva*. Fortunate are those who have the *zechus* to return to our Father in Heaven in these difficult days. They are spared from harsh *gezairos* in the material and spiritual spheres.

Ima: Are you also judged on *Rosh Hashanah*?

Galia: My dear Ima, every single soul passes before Hashem on the day of *Rosh Hashanah*, and every soul is judged. My own soul as well, despite the fact that I have no sins. They weigh the messages that I have passed onto you and check how many people have done *teshuva*. Then they register the *zechuyos* to our credits.

✣ *Yom Kippur*

Ima: Galia, last year, after *Yom Kippur*, you said that, "The prayers did not fulfill their need, there wasn't enough broken-heartedness, not enough love of Hashem, not enough truth, not enough desire to change. Ima, how will it turn out? Everyone can see that our Father in Heaven cannot allow his children to go on like this." Galia, what do you say after *Yom Kippur* this year?

Galia: Ima, there were more prayers and supplications this year, but it is still far from what it needs to be. *B'ezras Hashem* we will be redeemed on the basis of our *ma'asim tovim* and *mitzvos* and fulfillment of our Torah; Amen!

✣ *Succos*

Galia: The festival of *Succos* is a very special festival. A very great *kedusha* comes down to this world on *Succos*.

In the depths of their souls, people feel that these times are not normal, but everything is going to change. People will want to hear the word of Hashem. It is very important for people to take advantage of this because it's a great time of good will and hearts are open as never before.

There's a lot of joy in fulfilling the *mitzva* of the *succa* properly. It's a very deep matter, the main aspect of which, apart from remembering the miracles performed, is the protection from evil.

Ima: I had a dream that we put up a *succa* and we sat in it with a lot of our friends.

Galia: Ima, the *succa* that Hashem is going to build for us is the eternal *succa* of King David, which will *b'ezras* Hashem be built very soon. Hashem will give the *zechus* to all those who have worked hard for the sake of His Jewish people. They will see great acts of salvation and comfort, and He will reward them with fine and wonderful things without limit.

❧ *Chanuka*

Galia: Ima, you have to thank Hashem. The miracle of *Chanuka* reminds us of G-d's fantastic personal supervision of our lives that we have received throughout history. Very soon, with Hashem's help, miracles and wonders will happen whose meaning and greatness will be beyond our comprehension.

❧ *Eretz Yisroel and Torah — Jerusalem*

Ima: One day, I flew over Jerusalem and saw the Temple Mount from above. From the plane above, I saw how man is nothing. I couldn't even see him from high up. All the buildings are so small. Everything is so tiny and insignificant compared to Heaven, the planet Earth, all the galaxies, and the universe. So how is it that we, so tiny and insignificant, are important to Hashem?

Galia: Ima, we are perhaps small in terms of physical size, but not spiritually. It only looks like that in the world of falsity. You see a lot of falsity in this world. The site of the *Beis Hamikdash* and the Temple Mount is totally enraptured with a very high level of *kedusha*. A mighty *shefa* from the high places constantly flows through that place.

Ima: Why is it that one of the topics in prayer which makes me cry while praying is the part on Jerusalem, which is still destroyed?

Galia: Ima, because you are sad over the destruction of the *Beis Hamikdash* and the destroyed spiritual center of the Jewish people. It's like a body without a soul. How is it possible not to cry over a body whose soul has left it and is in such a terrible state? Can you see a body without a soul and not mourn over it?

❧ *The Kosel (Western Wall)*

Galia: Ima, the *Kosel* is wrapped in a precious light, which the eye of man cannot see or understand. It's a spiritual light, which exists there and feeds on the holiness of the prayers. Many souls of *tzadikim* are present there, and they plea in defense of the person who is in some form of pain or trouble, but does not know how to pray from the depths of his heart. They organize prayer in his mouth so that it will reach up and be accepted by the One who sits on high.

I do not have permission to specify any more or describe it verbally. Until the construction of the Temple, it is the holiest place to pray from the depths of your heart and ask for the acceptance of your prayer in the *zechus* of the

Shechina above the wall, both for your own benefit and that of the Jewish people. The *Shechina* never moves from the *Kosel*.

If people were to understand the greatness of prayer at the Wall, they would pray there from the depths of their heart. Prayers offered at the Wall are accepted more than from all the other holy sites.

I continually hope and pray that we get to see *Mashiach* and the construction of the *Beis Hamikdash* soon. The souls of the *tzadikim* of all the generations individually and together try to help the collective soul of the Jewish people. In these days we are so much in need of *mitzvos* and *zechuyos* to bring down the scales on the credit side so that there will be less *kitrug* against our nation, and less troubles.

Every *mitzva* which each and every Jew does reduces the trouble and helps us, as a nation, to make greater progress towards *Mashiach* the redeemer, who in the very near future will arrive *b'ezras Hashem*. The *ma'asim tovim* and the *mitzvos* of *Hashem Yisbarach* which we perform, will hasten *Mashiach's* revealation in the world and save us from sorrows and sicknesses.

❧ *The Blessing Of The Kohanim*

Ima: Can you explain the importance of the *Birkas Kohanim* in general and at the *Kosel* in particular?

Galia: Ima, the blessing of the *kohanim* is the last spiritual remnant left of the *Beis Hamikdash*. The Wall is the last physical remnant left of the *Beis Hamikdash*. The combination of the two is massive and extremely important. The *Birkas Kohanim* at the *Kosel* brings down mighty *shefa* to the individual and the nation. It's a great *zechus* for anyone to receive the blessing of the *kohanim* who function as a pipeline for the *shefa* which descends from Heaven to us on the material plane.

✣ *Palestinian Independence*

Ima: What is the significance of the fact that the Palestinians soon intend to declare an independent state?

Galia: Dear Ima, the Palestinians can declare what they want. "A man has many thoughts, but what Hashem decides counts." Even if they declare this, they will soon fall and be erased from the world.

No declaration by anybody is going to make any difference. In Heaven, it has been sealed that the Jewish people and the land of Israel and Jerusalem are one. Nobody can separate us from our land, our birthplace and Jerusalem, our eternal capital. It is the end of the period in which Yishmael has been allowed to rule. And like a wounded animal, he tries with all his strength to resist.

✣ *Tefillin And Tzitzis*

Galia: Dear Ima, you have to explain to people that a man needs to wear *tzitzis* all the time. That is the light that surrounds us and protects us from all evil.

Every prince bears the seal of the king. *Tzitzis* and *tefillin* are the seal of the King which a Jew wears to testify that he is the prince. When one wears *tefillin*, it is considered as though he has fulfilled the entire Torah. *Tefillin* are the signs which you have to observe, together with the sign of *Shabbos* and the sign of circumcision. It's a very great *zechus* to observe these signs, and doing so brings very great reward. This *mitzva* writes the name of Hashem on a person. The whole day, everywhere he goes, this Holy Name goes with him. Any evil that tries to get near and harm him is thrown backwards because of the holy and awesome name which is engraved on the *tzadik* who puts on tefillin each and every day. Ima, the *tefillin* that a person puts on have a fantastic power to bring down *shefa* to the world, to receive *kedusha ila'is* — a high holiness — and drive off and eliminate the forces of evil.

✺ *Mezuza*

Ima: Do you have anything to say about *mezuzos?*

Galia: The *kedusha* of a kosher mezuza protects the members of a household from the *mazikim* that lie in wait at the entrance.The *mazikim* are created by his sins.

You must be very wary of small *mezuzos* which have been casually written without holiness or sincerity. These *mezuzos* are written for material gain only and without the proper respect for a holy item. There are a lot of people who know how to write and are looking for easy money with little effort and write *mezuzos* with no regard, and sometimes in a way which is not kosher. Unfortunately, there are shops which sell people these *mezuzos*.

Heaven directs someone worthy of a good *mezuza* to buy a good, kosher *mezuza*. You have to be very careful of *mezuzos* written by female artists, where writing a *mezuza* is a hobby and no more.

You have to be careful to treat the *mezuza* with respect and check its kashrus from time to time, especially in damp areas. Dampness in the air erases and breaks letters and the *mezuza* becomes unfit and there is nothing to provide protection from the *mazikim* at the entrance to the home.

✺ Negel Vasser (The Pouring of Water Onto the Hands)

Ima: Maybe you can tell me why it is so important to pour water on your hands in the morning?

Galia: Ima, because washing *negel vasser* gets rid of the *tum'ah* of the night. It is very important to pour water on your hands because that way a man starts his day in a correct and efficient way without interferences.

✺ Birkas Hamazon (Grace After Meals)

Ima: What is the importance of *Birkas Hamazon*?

Galia: *Birkas Hamazon* is very important. It's not merely to thank Hashem, who in His mercy provides us with food, but you also have to know that through saying *Birkas Hamazon*, you are blessed with bounty from Hashem in every area. This is a big thing for souls who come to their *tikun* through the recital of a *bracha*.

You have to know how to distinguish between your physical appetite, which is for filling up your stomach with tasty food, and your spiritual appetite. A spiritual person eats to sustain himself in order to be able to go on studying Torah.

A true *tzadik* does not eat to get fat, but for the sustenance of his body so that he has a strong and healthy body to serve Hashem *Yisbarach*.

My dear Ima, the reason for the *mitzvos* is extremely deep and beyond our understanding and intellectual grasp. Only after 120 does the soul see the reward for the precious *mitzvos* the man did in this world of falsity. Fantastic surprises await us, those who fulfill *mitzvos* with devotion, love, and commitment.

& What's In a Name?

Ima: Maybe you can explain to me a little about a person's name. They say that a person already recieves his name in Heaven before he is born. His parents just decide to call him the same name he got in Heaven. It's considered a minor prophesy on the part of the parents. Does the name of a person have significance?

Galia: Ima, a person's name has a place in high roots. A person's name has great meaning. The whole character of a person is hidden in his name. Every name draws on its high roots like every tree draws from its low roots. In this world, a person personifies his name.

A person's name is selected in Heaven before his exit into the air of the world. He gets his name in Heaven and it just looks as though we are the ones who give the name. Heaven guides a person to give the right name to every baby.

Ima: What can you tell me about my name, Shulamit?

Galia: Ima, your name has a high, holy and special root. The meaning of your name testifies to peace, wholeness, perfection, and consummation. Shulamit in the *Song of Songs* represents the Jewish nation that is loved by Hashem.

Ima: What can you say about your name, Galia?

Galia: Ima, my name, Galia, says everything. It declares what my character is and my role in this world. To reveal the word of Hashem ["Galia" contains a root word meaning *to reveal*. See also below.]

Ima: Is it okay if people call themselves by a short name like, for example, Avi instead of Avraham, Itzik instead of Yitzhak? What should be said to people like this?

Galia: Ima, tell them that they should be called only by their full names. That way, they guard their souls from damage. The short name can cause defects to the soul.

The issue of names is much more complex than people think. All the letters of a person's name are in fact the limbs and organs of the soul which are spiritual.

[Note: In Hebrew, the letters of *Galia* can also spell out *Gila*, meaning joy. Another Hebrew word for joy is *simcha*, which was the name of my grandmother, *zichrona levracha*, and Galia is her reincarnation. Galia and Joy [Simcha] are in fact one and the same name — that is to say, one soul came to this world with the same name in two different *gilgulim*.]

❧ Sandak (The One Who Holds a Baby Boy at His Bris)

Ima: Are all the sins of a *sandak* pardoned?

Galia: It's a wonderful privilege to be a *sandak* because being a *sandak* atones for a man's sins, but only on condition that he decides to go on the straight path. Without that, being a *sandak* does not help. It's like the Day of Atonement which atones for the person who fasts and suffers and decides to go on the path of Hashem. But if that is not his intention, it won't help him and won't atone for him. Everything depends on the decision of the person to walk on the path of Hashem and fulfill the Torah and the *mitzvos*.

Ima: Why can't a woman be a *sandak,* like a man? That way her sins would also be atoned.

Galia: Ima, there are *mitzvos* only meant for men, and there are *mitzvos* meant only for women. Everyone comes to this world for the purpose of fulfilling his role. Women have certain roles, and men have different roles.

❧ The Holy Torah

Galia: The Torah was given as a present from Heaven through Hashem's love for us, and it is an asset worth more than gold. It is everything, and everything is in it for all worlds. There is unlimited spiritual pleasure to be had from our holy Torah, and we were worthy enough to receive it and must continue to prove ourselves worthy of receiving it.

Every Jew must study Torah. The Jewish nation exists in the *zechus* of our Torah and the whole world exists in the *zechus* of the Torah of the Jewish race. The more Torah, the better. The Torah is the soul of this world and this world is its material body. Ima, listening to Torah all the time is wonderful. It causes the soul amazing pleasure.

Ima: You once told me that you want to study Torah. Do you still want to?

Galia: Ima, I yearn to study Torah. I know you don't have time, but if you find a volunteer, I'll be very happy.

Ima: But even so, I will have to come along myself to facilitate the communication. And, apart from that, your soul knows everything. Does it not?

Galia: Even if my soul knows, it will make me very happy. It's a great spiritual pleasure to study Torah. Our holy Torah is for all the worlds, and it is beyond our understanding to comprehend this with the limited means of the mind. Only in the world of truth do you see the real truth and understand everything. In the world of truth, you get different tools for comprehension and knowledge, which a man does not have here. But they are tools which every soul has, and they can come into use only in the high worlds.

Ima, men must study Torah, because that is the only way that they can succeed in getting close to the Creator of the World. A woman is close to the Creator because of her nature and if she studies Torah, she gets even closer to the Creator of the World and has more enjoyment from this closeness to *Hashem Yisbarach* — our beloved King.

Ima: Do women receive reward for studying Torah, and going to Torah classes?

Galia: A woman also gets rewarded for the study of Torah. But it's calculated differently than for a man. Women also have very great reward in Heaven and are beloved to Hashem.

Ima: Is it all right for everything that you told me to be publicized? Are they not the secrets of Heaven?

Galia: Ima, there are no "secrets of Heaven." But there are secrets which just special people have the *zechus* to learn. That is the light I referred to, which is starting to be revealed in this world to the masses without them having to exert themselves so much. Hashem has mercy on His beloved people and is revealing the secrets of the Torah to them, because *HaKadosh Baruch Hu* in His goodness desires to redeem us from our troubles already and renew this world.

Ima, Hashem's Torah was given to us, only to the children He cherishes, and to no one else. We are the Chosen People because *HaKadosh Baruch Hu* chose us, but in the course of our history, we have disappointed our Father in Heaven. Hashem loves us despite everything because amongst the Jewish people there are pure *tzadikim* and people on such high levels that in their merit the whole nation is so beloved.

Ima: Why is it bad for a woman — and forbidden — for her to study *Kabala* and read the *Zohar*?

Galia: A woman has no business involving herself with that. Although women have extra understanding, they are light-headed and it is impossible for them to get involved with high things that demand an expansive mind. You can be damaged by dealing with something not suited to the vessel which contains it. The vessel could explode. It's like filling up a glass of water with a hose that supplies water at high pressure. The glass will break and the water will spill. The spiritual vessel is too small to contain all the *shefa* this deep pursuit brings.

Men who mix the secular and holy together can get very badly damaged spiritually and physically. These include men who get into *Kabala* and study high things before they have studied Talmud, *Torah she-baal peh*, the entire *Shas* and *poskim*, or those who say vulgar things, do not observe Torah and *mitzvos,* or study just for prestige.

Hashem and the Shechina

Ima: Can you explain to me what the *Shechina* is?

Galia: The *Shechina* is the love of Hashem for the Jewish people and it is with us all the time, but we, by our actions, distance it from us. Our prayers and keeping the *mitzvos* can help bring the *Shechina* closer to her precious people Israel. The *Shechina* is like the mother who longs to see her children. The prayer of any Jew has the power to raise up the *Shechina* from the dust.

Bechira — Free Choice

Ima: Galia, what's your opinion on free choice in this world? When you don't observe *mitzvos* you get punished. Do you call that free choice?

Galia: Ima, even so there is free choice. Everyone can choose to go the way of good or evil, but it is always recommended that one go in the way of Hashem. The fact that man can choose, that is free choice, but no one forces him to choose anything.

Ima: But if a person does not choose the good and the keeping of the *mitzvos*, then he will suffer. So it's obvious that he will want to choose *mitzvos* and that, in fact, is the negation of free choice.

Galia: My dear Ima, if that were the case, then everyone would choose *mitzvos*. But the fact is that the masses still do not keep the Torah and *mitzvos* properly. So is that free choice or not? You see yourself that it is. You can also do as you want. This is so despite the fact that all the years you know that good is bestowed upon those who go in the way of Hashem and evil is meted out for the person who does not keep the *mitzvos*. Often one chooses to fulfill the *mitzvos*. Sometimes, he does not. So, in reality you are free to do what you want. You have the ability to choose and act. All the same, only elevated souls who come with many *zechuyos* can choose to do things in the higher worlds, while others cannot, because choice does not exist there in the same way as it does in this world. When you reach the World of Truth after one hundred and twenty years, you will you understand this.

❧ *Hashem's Love for Us*

Ima: Hashem is so strong and great and mighty. It seems to me that Hashem is in a high place that is far off from humankind. How can he possibly be concerned for the welfare of each and every one of us?

Galia: Hashem himself relates directly to every detail of his creation. Hashem is in everyone. We are a part of him. Hashem is like a father, with a special love for each of his children. He loves each child individually. A person who really feels Hashem's presence is not afraid to ask him for something, because he feels how much Hashem loves him. Our father in Heaven looks after us all the time, uninterruptedly. He is always with us and we are never alone. Ima, Hashem has an unconditional love for us.

ᕱᕬ *Lighting Candles For Departed Tzadikim*

Ima: If we light candles very often for *tzadikim*, aren't we troubling and disturbing their peace?

Galia: No, the opposite is correct. If the one lighting the candle *le'ilui nishmas hatzadik* – for the elevation of the soul of the *tzadik* — is worthy, then the *tzadik* will plead for him and his prayer will be accepted. But a person should not pray *to* the *tzadik*, only *in the zechus of* the *tzadik*.

The candles that you light for *tzadikim* help you because the souls cast more light and can ask Heaven to have mercy on you, the person who lit the candle. Ima, a flame in this world has the power to light up in the higher spiritual worlds. The flames of physical candles have spiritual power.

Ima: When you light a candle for a departed soul — for example, for my late mother, *zichrona levracha* — does the soul know? Is it happy?

Galia: Ima, if you light a candle for a certain soul, it is happy and comes to help the one who has lit the candle. Family relatives who have departed from this world are happy that people remember them and light candles for them that raise them higher.

Ima: Galia, is lighting candles for the departed and mentioning their names before a Torah class regarded as an act of kindness (*chesed*)?

Galia: Ima, every soul that you mention experiences joy in Heaven. It is doing these souls a most noble act of kindness. They don't have the power to change their situation even one little bit. Only the living have the power to change their status.

Ima: Does it help if you mention the names of *tzadikim* in a time of trouble — even without lighting a candle?

Galia: Ima, saying the holy names of *tzadikim* can certainly help the one who says them.

Ima: When you light a candle for a departed and ask him for help, how can he help?

Galia: It is forbidden to ask anything from a departed person, even if he was the biggest *tzadik*. You have to ask Hashem that the mercy of Heaven be aroused for whatever purpose, in the merit of that *tzadik*. If the *tzadik* gets permission from Heaven, he can bring Heaven to have mercy on the living person, and pray for him so that Heaven fulfills his request if he has the *zechuyos* for this.

Sometimes you bless a person, like a critically ill person, but Heaven knows that he is a *rasha* and that all he does is anger Heaven; he is unworthy of mercy. In fact, the suffering that he is going through is atoning for his actions, and the *zechuyos* of his ancestors or relatives who are *tzadikim* are being used to protect him. The prayers of the souls of *tzadikim* can tip the scale towards the side of favor and ease the aspect of judgment set against him.

Ima: I can't understand what lighting a candle does for the departed. What power does the candle have?

Galia: Ima, fire is spiritual, and in the high worlds it can shine light on the soul. This is an act of charity for the soul and spirit of the departed. It's like the *mitzva* of giving charity. Lighting a *yahrzeit* candle to elevate the soul of the departed is considered to be an act of benevolence and kindness for it. If this is accompanied by studying *Tehillim* or Torah for the elevation of his soul, then the departed has permission to help by praying to Heaven, because then his prayer is heard and accepted, and that is the reason why you light candles for the departed.

✢ Non-Jews

Ima: Do you have a message for non-Jews?

Galia: My dear Ima, they too are people who are valued by Hashem. They are His creations and the work of His hands. He also waits for them to return to Him and fulfill the laws in which they are obligated.

All non-Jews are commanded and obligated to observe the Noahide Laws. They are all the progeny of Noach. It's important that they conduct themselves with fairness, honesty, righteousness and justice. Tell them that soon the world will come to its *geula* and consummation, and if they want to have a part of this, they have to work on themselves and improve their behavior and love the Jewish people, who are the Chosen People. Very soon, no one will have any doubts about this.

Ima: Is there some special value in the a non-Jew doing *teshuva*?

Galia: There is value in every person's *teshuva* and being aware and knowing that only Hashem is the King of the World. If they (non-Jews) undertake to perfect their *midos* and behave properly in all areas, they will get closer to our Father in Heaven. They will receive *zechuyos* for this, but the *zechuyos* they receive will be far less than those of the Jewish people.

Ima: Did non-Jews also come to this world to rectify their souls?

Galia: Ima, non-Jews are also souls who came to achieve rectification here, but they are in another category entirely.

The attitude toward them is entirely different; there is no basis for comparison.

Ima: Can non-Jews become *tzadikim*?

Galia: Dear Ima, they cannot be on our level. Righteous gentiles, though, gain a special *zechus* for saving the lives of Jews.

Ima: Is there some value in encouraging non-Jews to convert?

Galia: Ima, Judaism does not encourage others to convert. But we accept with blessing and love anyone who wants to convert. And if the person is genuine, he is accepted as a Jew in all aspects. In general, a person who converts is directed by Heaven to this path, because he has the spark of a Jewish soul, which got lost.

Chapter Ten:
Galia and Her Ima

"A mother's blessing has
the power to change the fate
of her sons and daughters.
If she is a mother who walks on the
path of Hashem, all of her blessings will
help her children dramatically."

Galia

Chapter Ten

❧ *Like A Field Of Anemones*

*I*ma: Galia, my little darling. The joy of my life. My life's happiness. You are the wonderful present which Hashem in His goodness sent me. You have succeeded in bringing spring into my life, all the wildflowers, chrysanthemums, waterfalls, and the *shefa* of light.

Galia: Ima, you brought spring to my soul. Again it is clean, pure and decorated like a field of wildflowers at the height of its blossoming. That's how my soul is decorated with your *mitzvos*, my dear Ima. Your love helps me to march on in life. All your spreading of Torah is wonderful for me. I am happy over this despite the fact that sometimes my life is a bit of a challenge for me.

Ima: Galia, everyone has difficulties in life. Everyone has difficulties of different types. There are some with health problems, some with financial concerns, old age; some need to find their mates. Everyone has his own special suffering.

Galia: Ima, that's right. But sometimes it's very difficult for me and I am in a bad mood; like now. It will pass. Generally, I can overcome it.

Ima: You are the one who is actually spreading Torah, because you are the calalyst that urges me on. You said that Heaven reduces the suffering of those who spread Torah. Is that true?

Galia: Ima, that's very true, and that is what is happening in my case. Your spreading of Torah helps me, too, and I suffer less. I could be suffering a lot more. So *baruch Hashem* that He gave me the *zechus* of your *mitzvos*. It's a big *zechus* for both me and you.

❧ *To Be a Normal Girl*

Ima: I wanted to tell you, Galia, that we will never have to separate because *Mashiach* is near and when he comes, people won't have to die.

Galia: Ima, when the *Mashiach* comes, I will be a regular and normal child like everyone. But no one knows if he'll have the *zechus* to see the *Mashiach*.

Ima: Why do I have to take the initiative and ask you questions, but you never take the initiative on your own to say anything to me? What will happen if all the questions run out? Will you not write anything?

Galia: Ima, you won't run out of questions. You'll always have new questions. And I don't take the initiative because I have no permission to take the initiative. I have permission to answer your questions but not to ask you. You have the *zechus* to ask and I have the *zechus* to answer and together, *b'ezras Hashem*, we can spread Torah.

Ima, you know how much I, your Galia, yearn to talk to you and tell you many things. But Heaven has ruled that I am in this false world with no free choice. I cannot initiate a conversation with you. What a shame that is, my dear mother! But I am delighted that you ask me so many questions, because in my answers I say things that I would have liked to initiate and say myself.

Ima: If you had the choice and you could start a conversation on your own initiative, what would you talk to me about?

Galia: I am not allowed to tell you what I am not allowed to talk to you about. Ima, you have to pray every single day and ask Hashem to send us His salvation quickly and cancel all the hard *gezairos*. Pray a lot. It's important to make a practice of praying everyday. It helps a person's *tikun*.

Ima: What helps one to get to a higher level of loving Hashem?

Galia: To constantly do things for the sake of Heaven and to pray meaningfully — that helps a tremendous amount. Ima, I love writing with you, even though I seem to be asleep. The soul never sleeps. It's wonderful for me to feel your happiness when you write with me.

✣ *The Dress*

Ima: Galia, when I went to the store to buy you a dress, I was so heartbroken over the fact that you are in such a terrible condition. I actually cried in the shop.

Galia: Ima, don't pity me.

Ima: How can I not pity you when you are in such a terrible condition? You can't even stand on your feet.

Galia: Ima, I'm not a pitiful thing, because I am at the end of my *tikun*. It is really you and all other physically able people who are still suffering. I just look like a pitiful thing. But I could say that it is you who are the poor things, because I am close to the truth and feel the love of our Father in Heaven every single minute, while you suffer from confusion. That's the worst suffering. No, I am not one to be pitied.

Ima: Why did I have so many problems before I became religious?

Galia: Everything is from Heaven. All the troubles of a person, in particular if he doesn't observe *mitzvos*, come in a chain, one after the other, in order to awaken him to do *teshuva* and good deeds. If he doesn't wake up, then he receives blows. Ima, you are fortunate that you woke up; otherwise you would have received difficult blows. When a person sins, he immediately creates an accuser for himself who has permission to harass him with all kinds of troubles and afflictions.

❧ *Bas-Mitzva*

Ima: Galia, soon you will be the age of a Bas Mitzva. What can I do to mark your Bas Mitzva and what type of present should I bring?

Galia: Ima, I have no joy from that because I am unable to become a true Bas Mitzva. I don't have the ability to fulfill any of the *mitzvos* of the Torah. So how can you celebrate a Bas Mitzva without the ability to keep *mitzvos*? But I am thrilled over the fact that I give you the opportunity to spread Torah, and this is a great *zechus* which has fallen to our lot. My dear, beloved Ima, the greatest joy for me is to be with you, and the book which you are writing about me is the most beautiful present that you can give to me.

✤ *Passed Out*

Ima: Galia, how do you feel now and why did you pass out on *Shabbos*?

Galia: Ima, today I'm perfectly fine, *baruch Hashem*. Everything which happens to us is from Heaven and is controlled by Heaven and we have no control over this at all.

Ima: A seizure and passing out is terrible suffering, is it not?

Galia: Ima, that's right. I have no control over my body and my body has no balance, because my brain, which is the center, doesn't function that well. It doesn't relay the right commands to my body, and my whole body goes out of control. It's terrible suffering for my body.

Ima: When I left your side to call an ambulance and prepare things to take to the hospital, why did you tell me not to leave you alone even for a moment?

Galia: Ima, you are my *tzadekes* and you do everything for me. But when I pass out, you have to constantly watch to assure that my tongue doesn't get swallowed because I can suffocate. You have to make sure that I am on my side all the time, until it passes. Until the attack is over, you should not leave me even for a moment because it's a life and death situation.

Ima: What can I do for you to prevent situations like this?

Galia: My dear Ima, you can pray for me.

Ima: When it happened to you, I said the *Shema*. Did it help you?

Galia: Ima, that helped me a great deal. Your saying *Tehillim* was also a help. *Tehillim* opens up the gates of mercy, and help a person a great deal in a time of danger.

Ima: On Friday, you told me you wanted to be a normal girl, to talk freely, to go for walks with me. Is that the reason you cried on Friday and told me you were attached to me and wanted to be at home with me all the time? I want to tell you, my precious Galia, that if I had the physical and psychological strength, I would keep you at home all the time, but I don't. If I had the financial means, I would hire a permanent caregiver for you.

Galia: My dear, beloved Ima. I told you these things because sometimes my condition is too much to bear, but then I manage to get on top of it and carry on. I want to tell you that this ability to manage is greatly due to you.

Ima: What was the reason that you didn't want to eat on *Shabbos*?

Galia: My dear Ima, sometimes I don't eat because my body gets so satisfied, it creates difficulty for my soul. I want to purify my soul as much as possible and being satisfied all the time doesn't purify.

Ima: Does the soul decide whether the body eats or not? Is the soul the supervisor of the body?

Galia: Ima, the soul tells the body what to do. Sometimes the body resists because it has powerful desires. Then it has a war with the *yetzer hora*, and in the end you see who wins.

Ima: Do you like to come home, even though I'm so busy at home?

Galia: Ima, it's not important to me that you're busy. Being with you gives me fantastic pleasure. They look after me very well here [in the resident home], but you give me true love and that's what stimulates me to keep going.

✿ Great Loneliness

Ima: Why are you crying? Are you sad about something perhaps?

Galia: My dear Ima (*Galia cries*), I am very sad because *Shabbos* is getting near and I am here all alone without my dear Ima. I grow stronger all the time through the love that you give me. You, my faithful mother, see to my needs all the time and visit me, but I miss you so much of the time. I am extremely lonely here, staying here without Ima, even though the attention given here is very dedicated. I long for your love, my dear, beloved Ima, so much. The hardest times for me are the *Shabbosim* here. (*Galia cries a lot*) Ima, I understand you very well and I know you don't have enough strength for everything.

Ima: Would you rather that I spend less time spreading Torah and have you home more?

Galia: Ima, your spreading Torah raises my spiritual level very much, and it's worth more to me than taking me home. But still understand, dear Ima, that I am very lonely here (*Galia cries terribly*). It's very sad for a girl to be without her mother for so many years. Ima, don't take it to heart, because my mood will change soon. I'll go to sleep and I will go on a trip around the high worlds and I won't feel the terrible sadness I have in this world that is my lot. I accept everything with great love, because Heaven is purifying me. This is better than suffering in the next world. Here it's easier to bear the pain and suffering (*Galia cries profusely*).

Ima: Are you so sad because I'm not with you all the time?

Galia: Very, very sad. Sometimes, it gets too much and then I cry. But normally I can get ahold of myself.

Ima: I love you very much, Galia. I spoke about you on the radio in Jerusalem and also in talks I gave this week.

Galia: All of your spreading of Torah is wonderful for me. I am happy over this despite the fact that sometimes my life is a little difficult for me.

Ima: Galia, Hashem gave you a mother that can communicate with you because Hashem knows that you deserve it because of your great virtue. Otherwise, you wouldn't get such a mother. Right?

Galia: Ima, you're right. And you know that Hashem is the perfect judge and gives everyone according to his actions. Ima, you are the delight of my whole life in this world. I know how difficult life is for you, but it will be worth your while after one hundred and twenty years, because in the end all that is left is a person's *ma'asim tovim,* which he can take with him to the high worlds, and there he can bask in them. Ima, it is worthwhile to concentrate on action in this world — *mitzvos* and *ma'asim tovim* — because we are short of time in this world, which passes like a fleeting shadow.

Ima: Before I became religious and before we started communicating, I had an inner feeling that you would save me from death, but I never understood logically how that could come about.

Galia: Ima, the feeling you had was correct. I really did, *baruch Hashem,* save you from spiritual death. I am your salvation and you are my salvation.

✎ *The Decorated Room*

Ima: Have you noticed the beautifully decorated room you've got? (I hung on the walls of Galia's room in her care center photos of ducks, teddy bears, and birds, etc.)

Galia: I want other photos. Photos of *tzadikim.* Of Grandpa and Grandma. Of Baba Sali. The Blessing of the Home. *Aishes Chayil.*

Ima: But I've got no time now. When I get the time or a holiday ... it'll take a little time.

Galia: Photos of *tzadikim*. There's no time!

Ima: No time for what?

Galia: Everything. These pictures cause me suffering. It's not kosher.

Ima: Galia, they're pictures of birds and animals. It's allowed to hang up pictures like these.

Galia: But it's not right for the Jewish soul.

Ima: It's a girls' room and the pictures are appropriate for girls of your age. (Galia was 10 when this conversation took place.)

Galia: Wrong. It's all right for non-Jews of my age.

(I took them all down and hung up pictures of *tzadikim*: the Lubavitcher Rebbe, Baba Sali, the Chafetz Chayim, *aleihem hashalom*, Rav Caduri, the text of *Aishes Chayil*, the Blessing of the Home, *Shema Yisrael*, *Modeh Ani*, etc. Galia radiated happiness.)

✌ *Galia Criticizes An Article In Ma'ariv*

Ima: An article which was published in the newspaper *Ma'ariv* [a major Israeli daily] on 9/19/96 about your care center stated: "Only at the end of my visit, in one of the residential areas, in the prettiest room in the home, did I finally meet the parents. *TO MY SWEET GALIA, FROM IMA, WITH LOVE* ... that's all that was written on the series of carefully painted pictures hung over the bed. I became choked up, because of the realization that all of the terrible and painful sights which I had seen in the course of the day ... these are are actually someone's children ... because of the understanding that loving them and living with them are not always things which necessarily go together."

I went over the last two lines and said to Galia, "That's very touching, isn't it?"

Galia: Yes. But the journalist doesn't understand what in fact is the love of a parent and what the love of our Father in Heaven is. It hurts me, this article. It's bad that these silly pictures represent love to her. She doesn't understand that when you hung them up, you loved me less. Now I have your whole heart. You don't need pictures when you have me, Galia, your daughter.

She doesn't understand that all the parents, with pictures or without them, suffer. They love and want their children healthy and whole. But Hashem is testing them.

Ima: I am moved by the fact that at last I have a true daughter.

Galia: That's the mistake of everyone. We brain-damaged have always been true children but only very special parents feel this.

Ima: They felt this without being able to communicate?

Galia: Yes. There are parents who feel this without being able to communicate.

❧ *Zechus Avos*

Ima: Is *zechus avos* that parents and grandparents give their *zechuyos* to their children? If so, what are they left with for themselves?

Galia: Parents pass on to to the person who has *zechus avos, zechuyos* which they don't need at all for themselves and which are simply surplus for them. It's like someone who owns millions of gorgeous apples and during the whole of his life, all he can eat is a few thousand apples. What does he need all those millions of apples for? He is happy to give them to others.

Chapter Eleven:
Galia Talks About FC

Ima, I feel that I am in
the world of the living again.
Communicating with you
gives me a link with this world.

Galia

Chapter Eleven

❧ *Our Early Communications*

Ima: Is communicating with you a form of prophecy?

Galia: Communicating with me and the brain-damaged is like prophecy, but not real prophecy. What is communicated are words that are said by Heaven. The Jewish people have to take them very seriously because they are the words of the living G-d.

Ima: Am I allowed to ask you anything I want?

Galia: Yes. You can ask anything, but I am not allowed to answer everything.

Ima: How will I succeed in learning how to communicate with you? I am trying but not always succeeding.

Galia: Be patient.

Ima: Do you know how to read?

Galia: Yes and no. Not like a normal person, because my brain is damaged. But my soul is perfect and knows everything.

Ima: Which of the weekly *parshios* — the weekly Torah readings, have I already read to you?

Galia: Stop testing me. This is not a test.

Ima: Am I talking to your brain or your soul?

Galia: You are always talking to my soul.

Ima: What is your medical problem?

Galia: Heaven has punished me. That's all there is to be said.

Ima: Why is it that when I kiss you, it seems that you don't seem to enjoy it? Don't you like kisses?

Galia: I like kisses a lot, but it's hard for me to respond.

Ima: Should I not kiss you anymore?

Galia: Ima, every kiss of yours saves me. Your love gives me the strength to continue. Ima, I feel that I am in the world of the living again. Communicating with you gives me a link with this world.

Ima: If someone were to communicate with you using a spelling board in English, could you write in English?

Galia: I know how to write in any language the facilitator knows. In the next world, there is only one language.

✢ Mother and Daughter and FC

Ima: Why can't I get the hang of communicating with you?

Galia: Ima, you just have to know that I want to communicate with you very much, because through that we'll get closer. But you need patience and and you need to ask the right questions.

Ima: Do you communicate with living souls only or also with dead souls?

Galia: With living ones. I receive messages from Hashem about souls in the next world. I have no association with souls who have left this world of falsity.

Ima: How is that you are sleeping and writing?

Galia: There's no connection between the two, because the inner being of all of us doesn't sleep and the outer being is linked to the facilitator. Ima, you are writing to my soul. The soul never sleeps.

Ima: In what way is the outer being linked to the facilitator?

Galia: The energy and technique of the facilitator activates our bodies.

Ima: What sort of person does the facilitator have to be to communicate?

Galia: A person with faith. But still, not everyone with faith succeeds as a facilitator. Also, Hashem chooses facilitators according to the individual needs of the people involved.

Ima: Is it possible to communicate with every child who is disabled with autism and mental incompetence?

Galia: Yes.

Ima: Do all mentally incompetent children understand things and simply look as though they do not understand?

Galia: Yes.

Ima: That's extraordinary. Really extraordinary.

Galia: What's extraordinary, Ima? My soul is just like your soul. It's just that I am in a limited body. The truth is that a healthy brain is also very limiting.

Ima: So you have a *zechus* in that you communicate — is that correct, Galia?

Galia: I have a *tikun* that is in need of completion.

Ima: Do you have to pass on the message you get when communicating or can you refuse to pass on the message?

Galia: I have to pass it on. I have no choice in this matter.

Ima: I also really want to write with you, Galia.

Galia: Ima, I am so happy that you are progressing toward the truth.

Ima: What is better for communicating, a small alphabet board or a big one?

Galia: It doesn't make any difference to me.

Ima: Do you have your own opinion about things?

Galia: Yes, but only to a small extent. It depends mostly on Heaven.

Ima: Does your communicating with me cause you any emotional or psychological difficulty?

Galia: No.

Ima: How can I make you happy?

Galia: Teach me Torah.

Ima: The angel teaches the whole Torah to the baby in the womb. So why do you need to study Torah? Don't you already know it?

Galia: I am a human being like you. The body needs kindness. Ima, help set up a yeshiva for girls, too.

Ima: A yeshiva where they study Torah through FC?

Galia: Yes.

✢⳽ *Discussing FC With Galia*

Ima: How do you manage to write on the alphabet board without looking at the letters? And you can even write while you're sleeping!

Galia: I feel the letters from the facilitator.

Ima: But you don't look at the letters.

Galia: Not with my eyes, but I do feel them.

Ima: How can I communicate on a deep level with you, like the facilitator?

Galia: Through a lot of *teshuva,* and a lot of work on yourself, and also through communicating with children.

Ima: Why are you hitting your neck? You've got a cut there!

Galia: I've got a cut because I can't control my movements very well.

Ima: Why is it that today you had to push your hand so hard?

Galia: Because I'm so happy to write with you, to tell you that I love you, to tell you that you are going on the right path, Ima. Don't be afraid of anything.

Ima: Is communicating with other children — obviously, with the permission of their parents — doing them a kindness?

Galia: Ima, communicating with these children is doing them a tremendous kindness.

Ima: How can I know when you really want to communicate with me? Do you have some sign?

Galia: If I want to communicate with you, you will feel it.

Ima: How is it that all children who communicate say similar things? Do they receive information from the same source?

Galia: Ima, all the children say the same thing because they all get their information from Heaven. Because that's what Hashem tells them to say.

Ima: Do you like to communicate with me? What does it do for you?

Galia: Ima, I really like to communicate because it gives me a feeling of belonging to this world.

Ima: Why are you pushing and pulling your hand? Do you not want to write today?

Galia: I want to write with you, but I don't have very good control of my body. Ima, I love to write with you. I want to tell you that you are a wonderful mother.

Ima: Tell me, Galia, could I pick up what you want to tell me without this communicating with the alphabet board? Can you transmit messages straight to my head, to my thoughts? I heard that one child communicates with his father like that. The father is in the United States and the child is in Israel.

Galia: Ima, yes I can. But it'll be more complicated for you because you won't be sure of what I am saying. But by grasping my finger, you can be sure that I am doing the writing.

Ima: Why are you hitting the board so hard with your finger?

Galia: Because I am very happy to write to you. It's exciting for me every time. Ima, you give me joy! I enjoy writing with you even if I am sleeping. It's wonderful to feel your happiness when you are writing with me.

✸ How Galia Benefits From the Communications

Ima: Galia, since I've been communicating with you, I am a new person. I am happier, calmer, more content. What does all this communicating do for you?

Galia: Ima, I feel that I am alive again in this world because of this communicating. Before, I felt like a dead person. Now I am alive again, and it's a great feeling to be alive. This communicating lets me feel like I am a living person who can express myself and have a two-way conversation, and that you, my dear mother, can finally talk with your daughter and your daughter can finally talk with Ima — that gives me a great feeling. Ima, you are the channel through which I pass information. You are also the channel whereby I am able to express myself. I enjoy it. Otherwise I am in a world of silence. You break this silence for me. It's extremely hard to be in a world of silence, without the ability to express myself. This communicating is like a tunnel of light for me. It is a way for me to call you, Ima. It's also a way for us to talk together about all the subjects of this world and of the next. So, Ima, our communicating gives me great happiness and it provides me with an opening to a beautiful world, to your world. Before I was cut off and now *baruch Hashem* I am part of your life and you are part of mine. Ima, I am happy over every letter I write to you. If you could see all the letters from a spiritual point of view, you would see that every letter I write you is completely dressed up in muslin and flutters and flies toward you, completely glowing with a precious light. Every letter has little wings which carry it to its target.

❧ Galia And Ima Talk About FC

Ima: Galia, do you want to write?

Galia: I always want to write with you.

Ima: Galia, could it be that part of this communicating comes partly from you and partly from me?

Galia: Ima, I am the one who is writing everything for you. It's just me, your Galia.

Ima: Galia, tell me. Everything that you're telling me — it's like being connected to the Internet, to a universal information bank that downloads information through a home computer.

Galia: Ima, I am connected to the holy light and Hashem provides a *shefa* of information for His creatures and that's how I know what to tell you. Everything depends on Hashem and everything comes from Hashem. Nothing comes from us. The source for all the information in the world is Divine.

Ima: Why are you holding back your hand? Perhaps you don't want to write today?

Galia: Ima, I always want to write, but my body does not always listen to me.

Ima: Can I put a question to you in thought as well? Or can I ask you only through the FC board?

Galia: Ima, you can think about the question and get an answer from me because my soul is not limited to physically hearing the question of the facilitator.

Ima: Before you pass on messages to me, do you get permission?

Galia: Ima, I don't say anything without the permission of Heaven. While you are asking your question, the voice of Heaven tells me what to say to you.

Ima: I'm not happy about troubling the voice of Heaven all the time.

Galia: Ima, you're not troubling anyone. I simply transfer the reply to you because every question already has its answer. It's hard for you to understand, but it's simple and not complicated, and the answer comes right away with every question and immediately presents itself. Sometimes I don't get permission to pass on the answer and then I don't pass it on.

Ima: Who gives or doesn't give you this permission?

Galia: Permission or refusal comes with the answer. You can't understand how this works in Heaven. It's beyond human understanding.

Ima: Is it all right if I communicate with you often? Does Heaven permit it?

Galia: Ima, I enjoy it a lot — and there's no prohibition for you to communicate with me; otherwise I would have told you. You wouldn't have been able to communicate with me if it was forbidden.

Ima: Does my communicating with you require a great deal of effort on your part? Does it tire you out?

Galia: Ima, my soul never tires. But the body, which is made of substance, tires. When it does, the soul, which is inside it, becomes uncomfortable and has to do what the body says and stop to let it rest.

Ima: Galia, why am I always so afraid that I will run out of questions to ask you?

Galia: Ima, because you don't how much time we have to communicate. You want to know as much as possible. You are afraid that what we are doing will come to an end. Dear mother, don't worry.

Ima: Galia, will this communication ever be proved to be authentic?

Galia: Not too long from now it will be shown to be authentic, and then people will relate to it differently.

Ima: How do you know these things?

Galia: I simply pass on the message to you from Heaven. I am just the pipeline through which this message is coming to you.

Ima: Galia, am I communicating only with your soul, or also with your mind?

Galia: Dear mother, your communicatioins with me are only with my soul because my mind is damaged and barely functions.

Ima: Lately I don't feel the need to write out complete messages to you because you already seem to know the end of the sentence without me writing it. What do you have to say about that?

Galia: Ima, you know this to be true in your soul. You feel my message. That's the reason that you don't need to finish the sentences. Our souls are joined together and you feel my messages.

Ima: Is it all right if sometimes I communicate with you while you are sleeping?

Galia: It's okay for me and if it's not, I'll tell you. Ima, you are the happiness of my life, and this communicating of ours causes me wonderful pleasure. Because, as you see, we can talk, even if not verbally. Hashem had mercy on the two of us and has allowed us to communicate as much as we like in our special way. So what if we talk in a way that is different from what people in this world are used to? The main thing is that we are able to communicate.

Ima: Galia, tell me. Do you write in Hebrew because you make use of my word knowledge, or do you write to me with these words because Heaven tells you to so that it will be understandable to all types of people?

Galia: Ima, I communicate with you in your words. The soul does not have actual words like people do. You have to understand that the soul knows everything. It doesn't have limitations in anything. A normal person has two windows — his eyes. I, Ima, have lots of windows.

Ima: One night, recently, I dreamed that I was dancing with a mentally incompetent child, but in my dream he didn't know how to dance. His feet hardly moved but he was very happy, and and the two of us laughed and were delighted.

Galia: Ima, that child is in fact your book, which talks about children with mental incompetence. You are a mouthpiece for us. The child in your dreams represents all those who are mentally incompetent. We are delighted that at last someone like you has taken the initiative to speak on our behalf, like an attorney who defends someone publicly, in front of others.

Ima: Galia, you know what's absurd about all this communicating? The fact that I am the mother and you are the daughter, I am normal and people term you as being limited; yet I am the one who feels inferior compared to you. Isn't that absurd?

Galia: Right, Ima. That's part of the falsity of this world.

Ima: Galia, the soul is above human intelligence. So how can the soul, which is from one dimension, converse with the mind, which is from another dimension? How can two different dimensions communicate with each other?

Galia: Ima, you don't have to strain yourself much to understand all this, because you cannot understand this form of communication with the tools available to the human mind. What you have is a spiritual dimension communicating with a material dimension, and the spiritual dimension passes on messages in a way that the material dimension can understand, even while the spiritual dimension understands the material dimension and the material dimension does not understand the spiritual. Ima, this communication works and succeeds on the basis of self-confidence. Any doubt, even the tiniest, on the part of the communicators, closes the channels.

Ima: At the beginning of our communications, what was the reason that you communicated short messages to me and wanted to end the sessions quickly and now, *baruch Hashem*, you communicate long messages and never ask to end off?

Galia: Dear Ima, I'm very glad that you came today. Ima, at the beginning you were taking your first steps. You can't jump and give an enormous amount of light to someone who has just spent an enormous amount of time in the dark. You had to understand and internalize things gradually, and I, too, was also more linked to my body, whereas now the fine thread that links me to my body has become looser.

Chapter Twelve: Bitter News, Uplifting Messages

The bitter news of
Galia's imminent parting came
at the same time that I was
completing my first book on Galia,
during a regular communication session.

Chapter Twelve

❧ *Learning To Say Goodbye*

The bitter news of Galia's imminent parting came during a regular communication session at the time of my finishing the composition of the first book on Galia.

Galia explained that we had to stop our intense communication, because we had attained the goal and fully achieved the purpose of the communication. There was no more need for these "crutches". We had to reduce and eventually stop the communication altogether, in order to make our imminent parting possible. The thinner the thread holding us together, the easier the separation would be.

It was hard for me to stop communicating with Galia. I was unable to give up my only link with her. I was ready to carry on communicating, even if that meant reducing my *zechuyos*, but Galia told me that a person should preserve his *zechuyos* at all times. Because the individual's *zechuyos* also belong to the Jews as a whole, and they add to the amount in the savings box, and when the box is full, the situation of the Jewish people is better. Everyone has to work on filling the boxes all the time with vast amounts and not take out anything, because times are hard and we need every coin and every cent in the box.

I continued praying to Hashem for the prolongation of the communication, and Galia wrote to me that the choice was mine: if I chose to carry on communicating for the welfare of the nation, she would also be happy to continue. It was all up to me, but I had to know that continued communication would make the imminent separation deeply painful. I chose, as you will understand, to continue communicating, for the sake of my beloved Jewish people and the spreading of Torah.

In order to prevent having to part from my cherished daughter, I tried to suggest to Galia that she ask Heaven to let her stay with me and become a normal girl, in return for which, the two of us will give up on all the *zechuyos* we have accumulated in this *gilgul*, and start to accumulate from scratch.

Galia replied that I can suggest and that she can agree, but that does not mean that Heaven will go along with it! Everything is done with the precise calculations of Heaven and with perfect justice.

We continued to communicate and when we had accumulated a large number of messages of staggering beauty and depth, Galia wrote to me that the two of us had received a further present from Heaven. Heaven would help me write a second book about her.

Galia further wrote to me that with the publication of the second book, they would interview me for the media. I included this prediction in the Hebrew edition of the second book. Following publication, the prediction came true.

When the book came out, I was interviewed in a live TV broadcast on the *Avraham and Yaakov* show (as previously mentioned). The show was aired on Channel 2 during prime time. According to the ratings, a million people watched the show. The interviewers were the famous TV personalities Kobi Midan and Avri Gilad, who had contacted me on their own initiative. A large newspaper feature immediately followed, and radio stations, both religious and non-religious, also widely reported the story, with a number of them interviewing me.

Galia then wrote that I would remarry very soon. She wrote the name of the man involved, and informed me that her parting was final, and that it would take place right after my wedding. Galia said in a communication with Rabbi Moshe Ben-Lulu, the director of the religious radio station, Channel 2000, that soon, *chas vechalila,* a terrible war would break out – and that we were about to go through a major, fateful change.

Knowing that publishing the book would bring the date of my daughter's end closer, I put off writing it. Galia pleaded with me and asked that I finish it quickly because it would free her from the cage of her hard life and the prison of her body.

Only after months of Galia pleading, persuading, asking, begging, strengthening, goading, encouraging, explaining and guiding, did I write the second *Galia,* named *Goodbye To Galia.*

It's astonishing to see the wonder of how Galia, a girl who is completely disabled, has co-written two books. What most completely healthy people don't manage to accomplish in a complete lifetime, Galia, the handicapped, brain-damaged child, did in a very short period of time. Galia is the materialization of the truth and the light that comes down from above. Isn't it a fantastic miracle? Hasn't the time arrived to search for the truth amid all the hidden falsity of our world, instead of surrendering to the rule of materialism and the prison of base desires?

Galia wrote that very soon, the whole picture will change completely and there will be very hard times for us, the beloved Jewish people, who haven't woken up enough. Nearly all of the

Jewish people do not keep Torah and *mitzvos*. It is still possible to return to our Father in Heaven. Now is a time of favor. But we cannot know how long this time of favor will last. We are the generation of the *Mashiach*, the generation of the *geula*. A generation that has the *zechus* to see open signs and wonders.

✣ *The Difficult News*

Ima: Galia, why are you so serious and so sad? You're really giving me heartache. (*Galia had already been terribly sad for an entire day.*)

Galia: Ima, I am not in a good mood. I can tell you that I won't be alive for much longer.

Ima: Is that the reason for you being in a bad mood? It can't be so; you're just writing that. What is this that you are suddenly writing to me?

(*I am simply unable to take her remark in.*)

Galia: Ima, don't worry. It won't happen quickly, but it also won't take too long. I have succeeded in inspiring you to become religious and to completely change. You are already managing fine without me.

Ima: Why are you suddenly writing things like this to me, Galia?

(*I am crying.*)

Galia: Ima, don't cry so, because I am also sad, even without your crying.

Ima: Galia, if you are sad and if remaining here depends on you, then stay with me longer.

Galia: Ima, it doesn't depend on me anymore. I have finished my *tikun*. You are my beloved mother. It's so hard for me to leave you, because only you are the one light of my life here in this world. You are the light which illuminates all this terrible darkness for me. But my soul is really waiting for the end of this terrible suffering in this world of falsity. Everything is so difficult for me here and makes me suffer. My whole situation and my terrible loneliness in this world are terrible. It's unbearable.

Ima: Galia, tell me that you're just writing all this. Galia, tell me that you don't mean what you are writing. OK? Galia, you give me strength. If you go, what's going to happen? How can I carry on? You are the center of my happiness. Yesterday, when you were unhappy, I couldn't function. Galia, you are my energy and my motivation — you are my happiness.

Galia: My dear, beloved Ima. You are the happiness of my life, the only one I have in the whole world. It's painful and sad for me to have to hurt you. I so much don't want to hurt you. I am telling you that I am extremely sad over the fact that we will have to separate so soon.

Ima: What does "soon" mean, Galia? Does Heaven allow you to tell me?

Galia: My dear Ima, Heaven told me to tell you, because you need to prepare yourself psychologically.

Ima: What can I do for you, to make it good for you so that you will be able to go on living with me for a long time? What can I do to provide you with a *zechus*? Tell me everything you want, but please don't leave me so quickly.

Galia: My dear Ima, everyone finishes his job here someday and carries on to another world. A beautiful, serene world where there isn't the terrible suffering that there is here. A world without alienation, without hypocrisy, a world full of great, true love. My dear Ima, my job ends with the completion of your book.

Ima: Then I think that I will never finish it. That way your job will never come to an end.

Galia: Ima, in finishing your precious book about me, you will give me a great *zechus*. It will take me up to the highest levels and dress me in a magnificent costume of staggering beauty. And regarding you, my dear mother, they still expect you to fulfill very important duties. Your *tikun* has still not come to an end. So, my dear Ima, carry on with your talks all the time. Don't stop, because that's my only request, that you go on telling about me and that way, I will accumulate more and more *zechuyos*. I will pray for you all the time in Heaven and will plead with Heaven to grant you all the best in everything.

Ima: Galia, but what if they don't want to hear about the subject anymore?

Galia: Ima, everything is directed by Heaven, and the only people who come to every talk or Torah class are those who need to be there, and are led there by Heaven. Also all your steps in giving talks are directed from above. So carry on with spreading Torah for my sake and for the sake of Heaven. Every book and talk that opens the eyes saves masses of Jews from catastrophes and all kinds of *gezairos* which, *chalila,* are decreed on the Jewish people when they don't keep Torah and *mitzvos*. My dear Ima, I will always accompany you with my presence and my love for you, because you and I are one.

Ima: Galia, what else can I do for you, to help you, so it'll be good for you, to make you happy?

Galia: My dear Ima, I told you that my happiness in life is your presence. When you are with me, I feel happy and protected, calm and loved. I am happy when I have permission from Heaven to accompany you spiritually to your holy work when you give talks.

Ima: But Galia, you know I am running around a lot because of the book and spreading Torah and also to give you a *zechus;* that's the reason why I have not been taking you home as much.

Galia: Ima, don't torment yourself because of that. I know about what you are doing for me and you have great reward for this in this world and the next world. I am extremely grateful to you Ima for everything that you do and have done for me. You worry about me all the time and have looked after me like the apple of your eye.

Ima: It's hard for me to accept this. You are my happiness, all the joy in my life. You know I am preparing a beautiful cover for your book. A cover full of flowers, because you brought the flowers and spring into my life. How can you write things like this (i.e., of your immediate death) to me?

Galia: Ima, you brought the spring to my soul. It is clean and pure again and decorated like a field of wildflowers, which you like so much when they are at the height of their flowering. That's how my soul is adorned with your *mitzvos.*

Ima: Ultimately, everyone goes back to the quarry from which he was hewn. But you told me that you will still communicate with me a lot [before Galia's death], and that you will pass on many deep messages.

Galia: Ima, you know that Heaven determines everything, including the time of a communication session and its content. I can still manage to communicate with you a lot and you can devote the coming period to giving me more of your time. I will communicate many beautiful, exciting things to you — obviously, with Heaven's permission.

Ima: Galia, will you let me know a short time before?

Galia: Ima, I am not allowed to tell you exactly, but I've told you to get ready psychologically, because we will not be speaking for a long time. Heaven directs your steps, as well as the time that you sit and communicate with me.

Ima: Galia, I need a lot of time to get ready psychologically. You're talking about something very difficult and I cannot psychologically prepare myself that quickly.

Galia: Ima, Heaven has also taken this into account. You
will succeed in coping because you have the mental
strength to remain strong even when things aren't easy
for you.

Ima: I really need to calm down. My Galia, what can I do
for you to make this easy for you?

Galia: My dear Ima, you have done everything that you were
able to do. Only the body suffers; the soul is happy to conclude its *tikun*. That is the main objective of people born
here. Heaven gives another chance to souls which have not
rectified the many sins of previous *gilgulim,* those who have
not followed the Torah which was given to *Bnei Yisrael.*

Ima: My beautiful Galia, what can I do for you? Would it
help if I pray for you so that you will not suffer so much?

Galia: Ima, there is nothing to be done more than what
you're doing. Anyone who hears you lecture, and who
reads your book and the messages in it, is brought to think
about Torah and learns to mend his ways. This is all that I
can hope for you to do for me. It brings me great happiness.

Ima: Do you intend to start eating too? Eat more.

Galia: Ima, I eat enough to keep my body going, but it
does not make me happy to eat. You know I don't enjoy
special foods or a lot of food.

❧ *The Shock*

Ima: My dear Galia, how are you and how do you feel?

Galia: Everything is fine with me, *baruch Hashem*. Don't
worry, Hashem looks after all his creations. Ima, stop crying

all the time, because it's terrible. You're really hurting me through it. I feel what you're feeling, and when Heaven allows, I am actually with your soul. I feel what you're going through from as close as could ever be possible, and know your thoughts and your happiness, and obviously your sadness. Every sorrow you have is also mine, and every sorrow I have is also yours, so, Ima, look after yourself. You have to understand that that's the way of the world — that in the end, everyone parts from this material world. We are not in control of ourselves to decide when we shall live or when we shall die.

Hashem dislikes when a person is sad and not happy, because when a person is sad or depressed, there is an opening for the *sitra achra* to take control. Happiness always drives away the pain and darkness from the soul. All the same, I feel that you are not digesting what I am saying. You don't want to understand, because no one likes bad or ugly things. In your mind, you constantly ask if Heaven allows me to tell you these difficult things. I want you to know that when Heaven forbids me to repeat something, then I don't. I only say what I am allowed t o. Heaven is taking pity on you and is allowing me to tell you important things such as these so that you can prepare yourself psychologically.

Ima: Clearly, our separation will be harder for me because I will remain cut off in this world of loneliness, while you are going to a perfect world, a world of harmony, joy and serenity.

Galia: Ima, physical separation from you is the most terrible thing for me. Because, you see, all these years, I was almost entirely in the next world. I was linked to this defective world only by a very fine thread, through my defective body.

Ima: Why did you want me to hurry up and finish the book if you knew that it would end your *tikun*? Do you want to end your *tikun*?

(Galia had been rushing me to finish the book about her.)

Galia: Ima, there is no soul which does not want to end its *tikun*. The greatest thing for a soul is to finish its *tikun* in the time allotted to it by Heaven. That's the reason why I have been rushing you this entire time. In doing so you will have provided me, yourself, and the Jewish people with the very great *zechus* of actually writing this book.

Ima: But that way you also shorten the time you can be with me.

Galia: That is correct, but it is also what Heaven has decided. Remember that completing a *tikun* is the object of all the souls in this world.

❧ To Pray For You

Ima: Galia, I will pray for you with all my heart and with tears and you certainly know that prayers can cancel *gezairos*. I will ask the Creator of the World to leave you with me a little longer. Will you agree to stay with me a little longer?

Galia: If Hashem accepts your prayer, it will mean the prolonging of my suffering in my body, which hardly functions to begin with. Ima, please don't pray for me to stay any longer than I need to.

Ima: Galia, I want to tell you that just recently, I started to understand how unfortunate you are in this life. I have just recently begun to realize. I had thought that that it would be better for you here in the care center, but I see now that from an emotional point of view, it is very difficult for you.

Galia: Ima, you're right. It's a very good place, but there is nothing like the love of an Ima and nothing is like a mother's care. Nothing in the world is equal to a wonderful Ima like you.

❧ Sadness In The Soul

Ima: If I cry and have great pain after our separation, will you also have great pain? Am I not allowed to cry in order not to hurt you?

Galia: Ima, you can cry, but as long as you are in pain, then I'm also in pain, and our pain causes pain for Hashem. When you find a way to overcome your pain, then it will be easier for us to part.

Ima: And if I will not have pain, then does that mean that you will have no pain?

Galia: No, it just means that it will make the parting easier.

Ima: I've never been good at saying goodbye. Parting has always been difficult for me.

Galia: Ima, it's hard for most people; it is very hard to part with someone.

Ima: They say that during the *shiva*, the soul leaves the grave to go to the home where it lived and from the home to the grave, again and again every day of the *shiva*. Will your soul, after one hundred and twenty years, go to the care center or to my home?

Galia: Ima, it depends. Each case is judged according to the person's *maasim*, *zechuyos*, and sins. There are souls who go straight to the court in Heaven where, on the basis of their actions, and the Torah they studied, are immediately punished or admitted to *Gan Eden*. Such a soul has no business in his home or any other home, unless he is a sould who can get an *aliyas neshama* [a benefit to the soul] by returning to the house of *shiva* and hearing *kaddish* recited for it.

Ima: Why do they say that during the first whole year after the departure of the soul, the soul rises and descends, rises and descends, and then only rises and no longer descends when the year is over?

Galia: My dear Ima, even for the worst Jewish *rashaim*, the longest period in *Gehinom* is twelve months. Part of the soul's suffering during this twelve-month period is to see that it failed to learn to rectify its ways through Torah and *mitzvos*, that it occupied itself mainly with empty actions that had no purpose. Then the soul sees the spiritual ecstasy that it would have achieved had it guarded the glory of Hashem. So during this period before the court sentence, it mourns over the parting with the people it loved and the parting with its material body which, when it was inside it, did things and deeds which it shouldn't have done. Then, it goes down and sees its pitiful body that served it faithfully. Once, so beautiful and alive, the body has suddenly changed its appearance, and this is a difficult sight for the soul to witness.

Then it goes up and calms down in the serenity, the glory, the brilliance, and the unlimited beauty in the next world. It then goes down again to become improved a little through this pain, and again its sins hurt it, and it goes up again and down again until the first rectification is over.

❧ At The Time Of Death

Ima: Does the wasting away of the body in the ground give the soul the right to rise with the dead?

Galia: Everyone has a bone called the *luz* bone. If a person has earned the *zechus* through his deeds, a new, refined and pure body will grow from this bone at the time of the resurrection of the dead and the regrowth of the living body will start from that bone.

Ima: But, Galia, how about someone who is a *tzadekes*

like yourself, who has never sinned, not in speech, nor thought or deed. Will your body remain intact?

Galia: Ima, we don't know that in advance. That becomes known only after one's death.

❧ *Pain Of Parting*

Ima: Your fate is hard for me to understand. You are a *tzadekes* and you have never done anything wrong. You have only done good and you help. Look, you got me to do *teshuva*. What a *tzadekes* you are! What *zechuyos* you have in Heaven!

Galia: Ima, I know that I have *zechuyos*, and I also know that the only person who cares for me and who is sad for me in this world, is you. But the main thing is that you don't get broken, Ima. Prepare yourself. Your book will give me, you, and all the Jews many *zechusim*. I will be able to go up to Heaven clean, pure, bright, glowing in a trove of *mitzvos*. I will be able to put on beautiful, adorned clothes in the high world whose beauty you cannot even begin to imagine. In this world, there aren't any clothes which can even compare to the beauty of the clothes in the high worlds.

❧ *What Can Be Done for You?*

Ima: Have they shown you your place in Heaven? Will you be there with my mother, *zichrona levracha*?

Galia: My dear Ima, don't worry. They don't leave you by yourself in Heaven. There is no such thing. Loneliness and isolation only exist in this world. The next world is completely full of joy, serenity and love.

Ima: I strongly hope that after one hundred and twenty years, I will be in Heaven with my mother and with you and with a number of other relatives that I love. Will they take this wish into account when it is time for me to go to Heaven?

Galia: The lot of everyone in Heaven depends on his or her *zechuyos*.

❧ *Auras*

Ima: Galia, I heard a certain rabbi speaks about auras. He said that an aura is made of light and leaves the body a little before the departure of the soul, and the soul dresses itself in the aura as soon as it dies. If that's the case, then the soul is not left bereft of a body for a minute, right? It has the aura in which it dresses, and I understood that afterwards, the soul gets other coverings based on its deeds in this world.

Galia: As I told you, every world has its own special clothing, because that clothing is appropriate for the conditions of that world. In the next world, a world which is all light, there is a special covering, a covering of light made up of the *mitzvos* of that particular person.

❧ *Departure Of The Soul*

Ima: They say that when the soul leaves the body, its voice is heard from one end of the world to the other, and we just don't hear. Does the soul suffer such great pain in leaving? What is more painful for the soul, leaving the body or leaving behind family?

Galia: It's all as I already explained to you. It depends on the person and his deeds. The pain of the soul is beyond all comprehension with the faculties that you have. It's a combined pain that includes the two things together. But the soul is not left alone with its pain. Service angels accompany it (or it could be angels of destruction, if that's what it deserves), and they calm it down and encourage it. If it is the soul of a *tzadik*, it has permission to rise up to the heights and spread out and have joy and delight.

You worry all the time. Ima, don't worry so much. I am going to the perfect world. I will have magnificent palaces surrounded by spiritual crystal and shining, radiant lights. And everything there is so colorful and beautiful. All the possible perfumed fragrances waft in the spiritual air I will have there. I will have adornments and magnificent costumes, clothes and radiant jewels and limitless, countless flowers. Everwhere are angels playing instruments and singing. The happiness is enormous.

Ima, if even one angel of the masses of angels that I will have in my world were to appear in this world, people would die just from the pleasure of seeing him or hearing his song. I am privileged, *baruch Hashem*, because I will have masses of choirs and angels playing music and giving off exquisite light [*noga ve-or yekaros*] and melodies and perfumes and flowers and trees, and everything there is so wonderful.

My *tikun* has ended here and it has ended in the best way possible. I was privileged to get you and many others to do *teshuva*. All this was accomplished without having the ability to speak or nod my head like a normal person. I also stopped you from marrying an unsuitable man, and now, *baruch Hashem*, you're on your feet and running and spreading Torah in your own right. Heaven is in the process of sending you a wonderful marriage partner who will help you in life and with your campaign of spreading Torah.

Ima: But Galia, I'm still not ready for the separation. I still can't accept it. How can you accept something like that?

Galia: Ima, you have to work on yourself, because that's the reason they revealed it to you, so that you will work on yourself. Otherwise there is no point. My dear Ima, please! I, your Galia, who loves you, ask you to think about it every day. Think that that this is the way of the world. Our goal is to complete our *tikun* here and part with this world and our dear family and reach that quarry from which we were hewn. Ima, don't take these things too hard. It is the way of the world. Although there are some people who, because of their many sins, suffer in death, the physical and spiritual suffering they go through saves them from all evil and atones for their souls. It prepares the souls to receive all the *shefa* of light and the limitless good in the high worlds.

Ima, you have to understand that in Heaven, judgment and justice are true and absolute. Everyone has to go through what he has to go through only for his own good. The pain that the soul goes though depends on the actions that we do the entire time that we are inside the body. For one person, it may be easy and painless, but for someone else, who has sinned a lot, his body suffers a great deal when his soul departs. That's the preparation for the purification from sin and the cleansing which gets rid of the *klippos* created by his numerous sins. That is the preparation which will allow him to enter the court in Heaven.

Ima: What can you do in this world to help family relatives who have died?

Galia: The souls of the dead follow the living and pray for their sake that all should be good for them. Nothing the living can do can assist the souls of their dearly departed quite so much as the reading of *Tehillim* and doing *mitzvos* in their memory.

Some people prepare a magnificent grave with luxury marble and masses of flowers. but spiritually, it would be wonderful if they read *Tehillim* or study *Mishnayos* in order to provide an *aliya* to the *neshama* of the dead person. It gives great pleasure, impossible to describe, because no material thing can fulfill the role of what spirituality and *mitzvos* can do.

❧ *Psychological Preparation*

Ima: Galia, in a way I'm suppressing what you told me. I can't take it in. It's hard for me to even think about it.

Galia: Ima, you should. Start to think about it so that you don't get broken. Before any crisis or any change, we should prepare. A man psychologically prepares himself even before moving to a new apartment. So before a departure like this, and a parting so total like this one, a person must prepare himself, especially when he knows about it beforehand, like you do.

Ima: Galia, why are you so sad today and why were you so sad yesterday?

Galia: Ima, I am very sad because you still don't grasp and still haven't helped yourself enough to understand the meaning of our separation. It makes you sad and you cry in secret, even though I have explained to you why you are not allowed to be sad. It is hard for me to see you like this. Ima, please don't take it to heart so much. The end of my *tikun* here also means the end of my terrible suffering. I am awaiting the moment when Hashem will release me from all of my suffering.

Ima: Galia, you also shouldn't take my sadness to heart. Understand that it's very hard to digest something like this. Even with all my strong faith in Hashem and the justice of His actions, for me, as a mother, it is still very hard.

Galia: Ima, Heaven took that into account too and expects you to get over it and be strong.

Ima: Galia, I understand that someone who dies as a child appears in Heaven as a child. In the next world, do they treat someone who looks like a child properly?

Galia: Ima, there everything is different. It's another world, and all the rules there are different. Children there are also gigantic souls.

Ima: Why did I dream about you sitting in the home of my late mother, *zichrona levracha*? Won't you have your own home there?

Galia: Ima, is that what you dreamed? That is a good dream. Ima, please, prepare yourself.

Ima: How am I going to prepare myself? I don't even know how to prepare myself. I can't take it in, and I don't want to think about it. I have no time to think about it, and it's good that I have no time to think about it.

Galia: Ima, that is not good, because you'll end up a sad person. You *have* to prepare for it. I told you that everything is from Heaven. There's no such thing as having no time. Time is in the hands of Hashem and everything is just and programmed down to the last second.

Ima: Does a soul without anyone to mourn or grieve for it go straight up to the heights, or does it first mourn over its body?

Galia: Ima, it's very hard even for a soul with no one to mourn over it, because it has a big change with which it must cope. The body that it has known for years is gone, and the fact that no one is mourning over it is also sad for it, but on the whole, it is easier for this soul to go up to the high worlds.

Ima: Why is it so difficult for the soul to part with the body? After all, the body causes the soul problems all the time. The body is full of crude desires and wants the soul to sin. I had thought that maybe the soul gets used to the body but now I understand that because of the body, the soul can execute its *tikun*. Without the body, it would be impossible.

Galia: That is right, Ima. It's beautiful to see from the conclusions that you are forming how you are starting to understand higher things.

Ima: When a sinful soul sits there in the court of Heaven, miserable and forlorn, who is there to help it find comfort?

Galia: Ima, the passing of time, the saying of *Kaddish*, and the reciting of *Mishnayos* all help to provide comfort to the soul. When a sinful soul goes before the Heavenly Court, it is shown its soul and the souls of its children who didn't keep Torah and *mitzvos*. The Heavenly Court says to it: "Why didn't you teach them? Why didn't you keep the Torah? If you had kept *mitzvos* truthfully and faithfully, you would not have to receive severe punishments. Now look at what's in store for your children because they committed sins since you didn't teach them the truth." But when one says *Kaddish*, and the *Kaddish D'rabanan* in prayer or after a study period for the departed, then this protects the soul.

Ima: After the soul leaves the body, is it left alone? Is it dark for it there?

Galia: Ima, the soul is never alone. It is not dark for it there because when the soul leaves the body, it sees great lights which enrobe it with softness and warmth. Words cannot describe the love it receives from this. This is the divine light kept in store for the *tzadikim*. Heaven makes it easy for the *tzadikim* so that they complete their *tikun* quickly. Sometimes Heaven prolongs their suffering, because when they accept suffering lovingly, they atone for their family and for Jews as a whole.

Ima: Do you have any idea how I can prepare myself for this terrible parting? What can I tell myself to provide myself with the courage that I need?

Galia: You have to understand the nature of everyone's great *tikun* and the daily war with the *yetzer hora*. Only then, when you understand the good waiting for you after the suffering, will it be easier for you to prepare yourself psychologically. The more you accept the reality clearly and truly, the better off you will be; otherwise you will be in a sad state.

Ima: If it did depend on you, would you be prepared to stay with me a little longer?

Galia: Yes and no. It's hard to explain. It's a spiritual matter which is hard for you to understand as long as you are on the material plane. You are looking for Galia, your daughter, the one who is in a body, and that's why the parting is so difficult for you.

Ima: From the day you were born, from the day you came to the world, did your soul know that the end of your *tikun* would be the writing of my book about you?

Galia: Ima, the soul knew that that was the end of her *tikun*, in the anticipation that it would succeed in bringing you, and many others because of you, to do a full *teshuva*. So *baruch Hashem*, I have succeeded.

Ima: You know, I thought that if your life had not been so pathetic like this, I'd be prepared to give part of my life to you so that we wouldn't have to part so quickly.

Galia: Ima, I know how important I am to you. That was the big strength which kept me going and which continues to keep me going. The power of your love is extremely great and it motivates like a huge power-wheel that gives me the spiritual and material power to cope.

Ima: You told me once that everything is dynamic in Heaven, that everything changes and is liable to be changed. Maybe the date of your parting is liable to be changed? Maybe they'll put it off for you a little?

Galia: Dear Ima, I see how you try at all costs to draw it out so I'll be with you another day and another day. That's why I, too, am sad for you. You know that everything can change and there's no means of foreseeing how. Everything is in the hands of Heaven and Hashem shall decide what He will decide. We shall have to accept everything that he has decided lovingly. He alone is the Master of everything and he alone knows what is best for us.

Ima: How do you manage to overcome all these things? It's must be terribly hard, isn't it?

Galia: I succeed only because of my faith and the knowledge that *Hashem Yisbarach veyisaleh shemo* loves us very much and does it all only for our benefit. Someone with complete faith, who takes suffering lovingly, does not feel suffering at all.

ᴥ *Fear Of The Trial*

Ima: Galia, you are such a *tzadekes,* who has never done a sin the entire time that you have been alive, only *mitzvos* that give you *zechuyos.* So why do you tremble in fear of the day that you will die? And if you, who are a complete *tzadekes*, tremble from the day of death, what can we simple people say?

Galia: Ima, everyone has to tremble in fear of the day of his judgment and his sentence after his death. There, every little detail is taken into account, every thought, every word, every act. Everything is weighed up on the divine scales of justice, and it's all to calculate the reward or punishment which the soul will get. It's beneficial that a person is measured with such precision. This way we don't lose any of the reward to which we are entitled.

Everything is for our good, Ima. Fortunate are those who fulfill *mitzvos.* Not everyone placed in a physically handicapped state like me, and certainly not everyone with a healthy body and mind can know what his *zechuyos* and *chovos* are. That's why many of the messages given to those who are mentally incompetent and autistic like me are not passed on to normal people. The person who thinks that he is a *tzadik* has to check and test himself in case the *yetzer hora* is trying to confuse him into thinking that he is a good person, and that he is allowed to make mistakes from time to time. *HaKadosh Baruch Hu* makes a very exacting account with *tzadikim*.

So how can we not tremble before the court in Heaven? There, all of our acts, all that we said, all that we thought from the day that we were born is spread in front of us. How will we able to argue with the prosecutors that we ourselves have created with our sins? What will we say, then? Therefore, an ordinary person, who is not mentally disabled or autistic, who is in constant communication with Heaven, only a fine thread links his soul to his body, and he cannot know how the Heavenly court will reckon with him. He isn't aware of his *zechuyos* or *chovos* as far as Heaven is concerned.

What's more, there are also those who outwardly look like perfect *tzadikim*, but do things which should not be done. They talk badly about people, and blame others instead of examining themselves — and all of this is done under the guise of innocence. These people have to search their souls and prepare for the blow in the court of Heaven. They studied and knew what was allowed and what was forbidden, and even so were drawn toward the evil advice of the *yetzer hora* and failed to overcome it, even though they also had Torah and *mitzvos*.

"Infant taken captive" [*tinok shenishbah*] is a worn-out expression in the court of Heaven. The law recognizes that a person not brought up to observe *mitzvos* is blameless. He can claim he was, as it were, abducted at birth and raised in a non-Torah culture. However, this claim has now worn thin in Heaven, no doubt, because with the spread of the *teshuva* movement and the easy access to Torah education for adult beginners, the option of *teshuva* has become a fact of daily life. Although *HaKadosh Baruch Hu* loves and pities us and the attribute of mercy tries to justify the actions of the Jewish people, every Jew has to examine himself precisely and regret his bad deeds and thoughts. They have to tremble just from thinking about the trial in Heaven.

Ima: Galia, that is staggering! It is such a detailed message. When you talked about the court in Heaven, it seemed to me like I felt your trembling passing to my body. Did your body understand with its mind what you wrote?

Galia: Ima, I told you things received from the voice of Heaven — the *bas kol* — conveyed these things for you. In fact, my soul is already almost entirely in Heaven, but, even the fine thread which links my soul to my body feels the seriousness of these things.

Ima: You are a girl *tzadekes*. You only have good coming to you.

Galia: Ima, despite the fact that I am a *tzadekes,* it is only natural that I fear and tremble to face the Court of Heaven.

Ima: How could it be that all these years I did not see with such clarity your suffering and your terrible plight as I see them now? Maybe Heaven arranged that I would see it just now, so that I can reconcile myself to parting from you.

Galia: Ima, everything is from Heaven. They didn't want you to suffer because of me. Here in the home I have always felt an enormous amount of pain, loneliness, and isolation. Even though the place here is so good for children like me, I have been simply miserable. Only your visits open up a tunnel of light for me, and every time you come, the light breaks through again.

Ima: What will I do when I long to see you and you're not here anymore, and what will you do when you long for me?

Galia: If people long to see each other, Heaven gives them permission to meet in dreams. Ima, if you long to have a look at me, you can always look at the photos you took of me and I can see you practically anytime I want. You have to understand that I'm leaving my handicapped body, smitten by a blow from Heaven, but the soul never dies. That's a spiritual matter. Everything which becomes rectified goes back to its source.

Ima: Is the next world clearly visible like this world, or like in a dream?

Galia: Ima, this world is like in a dream in comparison with the next world. It is the next world that is the clear one.

Ima: Is everything there clear and bright? Not blurry and misty like in a dream?

Galia: The next world is the utimate clarity. The only mistiness is in this world. Because of the involvement of the *sitra achra,* who is appointed in charge of the *yetzer hora,* this world is simply unable to take in all the clarity and light. For different reasons, the forces of *tum'ah* are mixed in a dreamlike fashion, and that's why dreams aren't always clear. In the spiritual world, unlike in a dream, everything is clear.

Ima: Galia, I can't seem to understand this matter. This whole business of parting appears to me as though it is not about me at all. How can I take it in?

Galia: Ima, you are such a clever person. You understand everything, yet refuse to believe. You surround yourself with all kinds of reasons and excuses. You have to prepare yourself so that you won't get broken, because it will be difficult for you to part with me. This is the reason that I received Heaven's permission to inform you beforehand, so that you can prepare yourself and not get broken over it. Why don't you prepare yourself? There is not much time left and you have to prepare for it and recognize the reality.

Ima: You also have to stop being sad. Is there something I can do for you, to help you?

Galia: Nothing, Ima. I'm not really sad. Only complete faith and trust in Hashem can help. Throughout my life, you have done for me what only a dedicated Ima like you could do. You are my true, precious, and unceasing love. You never gave up on me. You always looked after me with such great dedication. You are the only one I love. Dear Ima, Heaven will reward you because you acted with such noble dedication, without limit. You did such a divine kindness to look after a girl in such a terrible physical state like mine. Even for an Ima, it's very hard. That is what makes your reward double and quadruple.

Ima: Galia, it's hard for me to see you sad. It breaks my heart. I ask again; how is it possible to make you happy?

Galia: Just strengthen yourself with true faith and reconciliation with reality. These days are extremely hard for me. It's hard for me to see you suffering. I am grateful to you and happy that you come to me all the time. But have courage, and believe with complete trust that all the actions of Hashem are for the good.

Ima: I am happy that you encourage me. But when I leave here or when I take you back to the center, I go back to being unreconciled with the situation. It's as though I don't want to understand. In fact, I am running *away* from reality. But what you say gives me new strength again and again.

Galia: Ima, always remember that I accept everything with great love. Hashem loves us and does everything for our good. Suffering in life and death are meant for a higher purpose, to enable a person to enter the perfect world. Ima, prepare yourself for our inevitable parting and be happy for my sake. It's a good idea to pray for the elevation of my soul. It's important to pray for the souls of the departed. It enables them to get much higher in Heaven and gives the souls of *tzadikim* the *zechus* to pray for the members of their family who are still alive, to plea for the Jewish people and for the cancellation of catastrophes and hard *gezairos*.

Ima: Why are you crying?

Galia: I'm crying about everything. About my situation and about the situation of the Jewish people as a whole. The believers and the servants of Hashem are the spiritual center of the Jewish people, and they are examined first. Tell everyone to do *teshuva* immediately because there is no time. In the near future, there will be a grand revelation.

Ima: Why do you cry so much? I'm really disturbed about your crying, and why you haven't eaten.

Galia: My dear Ima, I suffer much over my Jewish people who aren't following the right path and Hashem is angry with us. That's the reason that I am not in a good mood today. I am crying and don't want to eat, because I know what's going to happen to us soon. And it's really hard for us, for all of us, because we aren't going on the right path as much as we could be.

❧ Eternal Spring

Ima: Galia, how are you? How do you feel? How was it in the swimming pool? (*Astonishingly, Galia has learned to swim despite her condition. She swims really well and in deep water, and loves the water a great deal. This wonder can be observed on video.*)

Galia: Today I feel better and am smiling a lot. Ordinary people have no grasp or understanding. My body, too, has no ability to understand why I am smiling but I already explained to you that although only a fine thread links my soul to my body, sometimes the body still feels something of what the soul feels. I smiled outwardly, as though for no reason, but it was very pleasant for me in the water. It's very pleasant to be in the pool. It gives the body a feeling of floating in the air, reminiscent of the soaring of the soul in the high worlds.

In the water, the body feels a little of what the soul feels when in a high place. Cleanliness and purity in a place where there is quiet, rest, and eternal serenity without worries. It also shows the wonder and the supernal kindness that Hashem is doing for a girl like me and for other people who are mentally incompetent and autistic who have never learned to swim and yet remain above the water.

Ima: Galia, do swimming and the pleasure you get from being in the water make you forget a little of your suffering and your physical pain?

Galia: Ima, my suffering will also end soon. I will be starting a new chapter. My soul is starting to flower as though it were spring. It's going to be an eternal spring, which will never be followed by a summer, an autumn, or a winter. Everything will be spring: beautiful, adorned, and pleasant. The winter is behind me, the autumn is behind me, the weakening heat of the summer is behind me. The spring alone stands before me now. It's like swimming in clear, pleasant water, like the water that I enjoyed today in the pool.

Ima: If a person knows that death is just suffering that passes quickly and is in fact just a transition phase he goes through on the way to the perfect world, then it is easier for him to bear the suffering before the great happiness. It is really like labor pains. They make a woman suffer a lot, but the woman knows that in the end the suffering will lead to happiness. It seems to me that all the suffering of death is temporary and transient, like labor pains, and leads to a wonderful spiritual happiness in the high worlds.

Galia: Ima, your description is very accurate and close to reality. The suffering we experience helps us get to a wonderful place. It is simply the vehicle, not the goal. The goal is unlimited happiness. Suffering is the tunnel you have to go through in order to reach this unlimited pleasure. There is no other passageway. This is because of the sin of *Adam Harishon*.

✵ *Is Death Serenity?*

Ima: Why do they say that after the soul leaves the body, spiritual forces come to it and harass it?

Galia: It depends on the individual's actions. That doesn't happen to *tzadikim*. There are no destructive forces that come to them. Destructive forces come only to those people who did not keep Torah and *mitzvos* and thereby created *mashchisim* — destructive spirits. These same *mashchisim* come to them to exact payment from them on the day of judgment.

Ima: There are people who think that death is serenity and peace. I also thought so before I became religious. What can you say to these people?

Galia: Tell them that they are mistaken, that death is serenity only for the person who prepared for himself the means to receive that serenity. But the person who did not bother and did not prepare in this world has no serenity in the next world. It is, in fact, quite the opposite. The only serenity that he will have known will be whatever serenity he had in this world. For him, true suffering will begin only in the next world.

Ima: Is that so? These are very frightening things that you are saying.

Galia: It's forbidden to run away from reality. You have to struggle, face to face with reality, at all times.

Ima: Is it considered kindness to make people aware that they can do a kindness to their departed and give them the *zechus* of entry into the high worlds?

Galia: Ima, that is a very big kindness. If people would pray for their departed relatives and study *Mishnayos* or *Tehillim*, and donate charity in the name of the soul of the departed, and recite the *kaddish*, then they would be doing a lot for the souls of the departed and for the souls of the *rashaim* by saving them from the fires of *Gehinom*. There is no greater kindness than kindness to a dead person, because you don't expect him to give you anything back.

But, if the soul of the dead person prays to Heaven for the living, Heaven hears and accepts that prayer, and this is the reward that is received by the person who does kindness to a dead person. There are many souls who are in a very sad situation in the next world and they need every little bit of *mitzva* that you can give them. Kindness to the dead is a great thing for the Jewish nation and will give us *zechusim*.

Ima: How do you prepare yourself for all this? Can I learn from you?

Galia: Ima, I pray to Hashem. That's the best preparation.

Ima: I imagine that when the soul leaves the body, the curtain which cuts off its view in this world goes up and does not hide anything anymore and then it sees our material world without concealments. Is that right?

Galia: That's right, Ima. A soul outside the body has nothing hidden from it; it sees everything. It can see all of the secrets of the high worlds and also of these material worlds.

Ima: When a person cries over his departed — does that hurt the departed person?

Galia: Despite the fact that he is crying because he is in great sorrow and not because of any intention to hurt, it still hurts the departed person very much. The soul then sees the terrible pain of the person suffering more than he needs to. He causes himself physical damage and spiritual damage. It is easier for the *sitra achra* to rule over someone who is sad all the time. Sadness doesn't contribute anything to the elevation of the soul of the departed. If a person truly mourns over the death of a relative, instead of being overly sad, he should study Torah and read *Tehillim*. This will bring far more joy to the deceased and to Heaven.

You have to explain to people who go nearly every day to the cemetery to visit the graves of their dear departed that it's not good to bother the dead when it's not on the anniversary of the death or the general *kaddish*.

❧ *The Dinur River and the Suffering Of The Soul*

Ima: I read that every soul has to immerse in the Dinur river. Does this include *tzadikim*? What is the Dinur river? Is it a river of fire?

Galia: Ima, the Dinur river is like a ritual bath; it's like going to the *mikva* on *erev Shabbos*. After that, a person is ready to put on the spiritual costume that Heaven has prepared for him from the letters of the Torah that he had the *zechus* to study in life. Then everything is ready for receiving the *Shabbos*, as the next world is like *Shabbos*.

Ima: You told me that only a few special people know on which day they will die. Do you know?

Galia: Ima, I know the exact day, minute, and second.

Ima: Does it frighten you?

Galia: No, I am happy about the end of my *tikun* in this world of falsity. Someone who has complete faith in Hashem is not afraid of anything.

Ima: Is the time in this world the same time in the next world too?

Galia: Ima, time for the soul is completely different from time as you understand it in this world. In the spiritual world, all the concepts of time change beyond all recognition.

Ima: Does the body like to be in this world?

Galia: It's a punishment from the time of the expulsion of Adam and Chava from *Gan Eden*. Life here is full of suffering for the body, and that is its *tikun*.

Ima: I think it's possible to stand the pain of death because Hashem wouldn't cause pain that you could not stand up to.

Galia: Excellent, Ima. Right. But that doesn't detract anything from suffering. Outside the body, the soul has mighty abilities for enduring very great pain, which, sometimes, inside the body, the soul cannot stand at all.

Ima: They say that *Gan Eden* is is not actually trees and flowers and canopies but that it is just described like that so that people can understand, and that everything is in fact spiritual and impossible to grasp.

Galia: My dear Ima, I am happy that you asked a question and also gave a fine and very correct answer. Everything is spiritual. Everything is much higher than the material. It's a world which cannot be grasped by the brain of material man.

Ima: Are you allowed to ask for help after parting?

Galia: Ima, you may ask for help, but only from Hashem. You can add: May there be such and such (a request) in the *zechus* of certain *tzadikim*. But you may only ask things of the Master of the World.

✧ *End Of The Tikun*

Ima: I wanted to tell you, Galia, that our separation will leave me with an extremely large vacuum. I am completely incapable of thinking how I will be able to part with you. You are the center of my life. Lately, I have felt as though you are starting to move away from me. I think of how I'll long for you, to hug you, to see your smile. Your love and your smiles have given me so much strength in the last two years. My *teshuva* and the writing of this book have also given me new life, and all of this is because of you. I'll miss you so much. It's terrible to think about it. Who will fill the whole void?

Galia: My dear Ima, you won't feel a vacuum at all, because before our parting, you will meet the love of your heart (she wrote his name), and you'll get married quickly, and he will fill the vacuum.

This sadness of yours is just before a period of supreme blooming in your life waiting for you. It's like the sadness before the supreme blooming waiting for me in the next world, which is the perfect world. You can't even picture the beauty and the happiness waiting for me there, my dear Ima.

Ima: How do you know where you are going, to which place, and what you'll have there?

Galia: Dear Ima, souls know everything, and in the higher worlds, no one is ever left alone, the soul is always surrounded by great love, by angels the souls of *tzadikim* — if it has the *zechus*. I have had the *zechus* to see all which is waiting for me in the high worlds. And every time that I am once again shown those realms, it becomes easier for me for to be ready to part from this world of falsity.

Ima: They say that it is extremely difficult for the soul to part from the body, maybe because it succeeded in achieving its *tikun* through the body. I think that it's also extremely difficult for the body to part from the soul, because it is the soul that gives it all of its life. Without the soul, it has no life or any value at all.

Galia: Ima, that's an almost accurate description of the matter. That is in fact true that the soul does has life without the body. But the body materially helps the performance of *mitzvos* or sins, which, without the body, would be impossible for the neshama to accomplish. The body feels pain over parting with the soul because it served it for all of its life, while the soul feels pain over parting with the body, because with it, it succeeded in completing its *tikun*. Despite the fact that my body did not serve me in the way that a body generally serves most people, nonetheless my soul was able to achieve its *tikun* due to the fact that it was residing in my body.

Ima: After one hundred and twenty years, after we part, will you come just to me or will you also come to your father and brothers?

Galia: Ima, the soul goes to all of its family and dear ones. I love you all. Their souls will feel that I am among them, and it will be very sad because the soul knows everything and is aware of the loss.

Ima: What is the most difficult thing for you here in this world?

Galia: Ima, everything is difficult for me. My entire life on this planet is difficult for me, but above all I find it hard to be dependent on others.

Ima: Are you interested in listening to a tape of the rabbi's on death and the transition to the World of Truth?

Galia: It's a bit funny to have me listen to what a man who is still inside his body will tell me when I, from the day I was born, have existed in my soul, which effectively already resides in the higher worlds, with only a fine thread linking me to this world. I have first hand knowledge of these things, more than any book or tape. I see them spiritually, but I'll be happy to listen, if it will make you happy.

Ima: My dear Galia, from whom will you be sad to part? Which members of the family?

Galia: My dear Ima, what close family members say or put in words is not always what's in their heart. It's difficult for some of the family to accept that they have a relative with mental incompetence who looks like I do. But I do believe that when the day will come that will be the end of my role here, they will feel sad from the bottom of their hearts. I also feel that many people who know me from all the work that you have done will be sad at my parting from them.

❧ *Apology*

Ima: I want to ask an apology of you that I wasn't able, and I did not have enough physical and psychological strength, to bring you up and look after you at home. I also did not have enough money to pay for a person to care for you and be in your constant attendance. Do you forgive me?

Galia: Ima, of course, I forgive you for everything. In fact there is nothing for me to forgive. You dedicated your entire life to me and gave me so much love and warmth, with supreme dedication. What is there to forgive? I am grateful that you have always worried about me and that you came to visit me so often.

✧ Not To Communicate Anymore

Ima: You no longer have the need for communication sessions with me?

Galia: That's what Heaven has planned so that we can distance ourselves a little, because the link between us is very strong and it's very hard to break off. When we stop communicating, the link will weaken a little and that will assist us toward preparation for the final break. Ima, please try to cut down the degree of your communications with me until you get to a point where you cease communication with me. Cut down gradually, so that we can separate. This is all for your benefit. Go on rising in spirituality. You no longer need my help. I wish you success.

Ima: Will it do you good, if we stop communicating? Doesn't communicating help you too?

Galia: Ima, all this communicating is great for me. A major purpose of the communication was to pass information from Heaven to you so that you could write this book. This will assist many in coming to an understanding that there is life after death and someone who rules the world firmly and runs our lives. Everyone is subject to reward and punishment based on his *zechuyos* and *chovos*. But you don't need that (communication) anymore, and I will manage without it too. You have to understand that you must start to part from me, and stopping to communicate is part of the separation.

Ima: But if we continue communicating, that can bring people to do *teshuva*.

Galia: My dear Ima, that's a good argument. But we do not decide things. For your good, the best thing is to stop communicating with me, notwithstanding all the pain that is involved.

Ima: My dear Galia, you're making me feel emotional to the point of crying. You remind me of my mother. You are talking to me now the way a mother speaks to her child before they part.

Galia: Ima, maybe. But it is part of my *tikun* to tell you these things.

Ima: Galia, do thoughts have influence?

Galia: Ima, thought has massive powers. It can split the Heavens and reach the highest heights. There is such a thing is guarding one's thoughts. A man should purify his thoughts. You have to work on that too because thoughts have very strong powers to affect things spiritually. Thoughts can change spiritual processes in Heaven, and on earth between people. Everything that happens in this world is linked to spiritual worlds. It can connect to spiritual worlds both for good and, *chas vechalila*, for the bad. So you always have to drive out bad thoughts and try to think positively, so as not to let the *sitra achra* change a bad thought into a reality.

✣ *Continuing To Communicate*

Ima: Galia, what do you say about continuing to communicate like always, even if it will be harder and more painful? I am prepared. Are you also prepared? It can be a *zechus* for the public because the things you say strengthen people very much.

Galia: Like I told you, I agree despite the fact that our continuing to communicate now will make the final separation much more difficult for you. Nonetheless, the final decision rests with you. You have to make the decision.

Ima: Galia, I've decided. I agree to everything for the sake of Torah and to bring the Jewish people to do *teshuva*. I am lovingly ready to do this for Heaven's sake and for His name, even if afterwards I will suffer pain in parting with you. Are you ready?

Galia: Ima, I told you that I agree. Ima, Heaven had mercy on you, so that the parting should not be too difficult for you. If you are ready to take upon yourself the enormous difficulty which you'll have in parting with me, then we'll carry on communicating, for the sake of our precious Jewish people, so that they will do *teshuva* en masse. I will do everything that I can for my beloved Jewish people, because I know that the that things I say enter their hearts.

Ima. I am almost completely outside the body and see that everything has been prepared for me. *Baruch Hashem* that I have gained a wonderful lot such as this. A major portion of it is due to you, that you helped me rectify my soul and consummate it. I am glowing all over, sparkling with a display of glowing lights. Ima, every moment in the spiritual world is full of pleasure. Even if a man were to live two hundred years of pleasure in the material world, those years in this world would not compare with just one happy moment in the next world.

✌ *Media Interview*

Galia: Ima, in a little while, after you finish your book, you will begin to speak to the media. The words that will be spoken by you from the bottom of your heart will persuade many to think about *teshuva*. It will all happen soon. At the moment, you may have a break from it, because you have to concentrate on the book. Heaven has arranged it that they won't turn to you yet. But get ready, my beloved Ima. When your next book about me comes out, *b'ezras Hashem Yisbarach*, you will be given offers from all angles to be interviewed by the media.

✌ Teshuva

Ima: Galia, was it hard work for you to get me to *teshuva*?

Galia: Yes, Ima. Very hard. I had to work extremely hard to break the shell, but I knew that it was well worth the effort.

Ima: If I hadn't done *teshuva*, would you have gone on living and suffering for a longer time? Would the suffering itself have been the rectification that you needed?

Galia: If you hadn't done *teshuva* or if you married that unsuitable person, my suffering would have been extemely intense and it definitely would have lasted longer. But it is also possible that I would not have succeeded in achieving my *tikun* in this *gilgul*. I would have lost you and you would have had to pay very dearly for it.

Ima: Would you have had to come back in another *gilgul*?

Galia: Almost certainly yes.

Ima: Does it seem to you that I have completed my *teshuva*?

Galia: You have to do *teshuva* all your life. We all have to do *teshuva* our entire lives.

Ima: Did you know from the outset that you would succeed in getting me to do *teshuva*?

Galia: Yes. That was the role assigned to me in this world. But it was up to you to decide whether to do so or not. *Baruch Hashem* that I had the *zechus* to wake you up from your deep sleep. I give thanks to Hashem who gave you the *zechus* to wake up. My dear mother, you have done *teshuva*, and I have completed my mission to get you to do *teshuva*. In doing so, I have rectified you, my soul, and masses of Jewish people. Your book about me will complete the whole picture and get many to do *teshuva*. It will open the eyes of all those who think that this material world is just about material pleasures and that Torah and *mitzvos* have nothing to do with them. When the eyes of those who read the book will be opened up and they will understand that there is reward and punishment, then I will be able to reach the perfect place. Then my *tikun* will be considered complete.

✢ Requests

Ima: Galia, I turn to you again and tell you to ask me whatever you like and I'll try to do it for you.

Galia: Ima, nothing at all. I do not have anything to ask of you. You have done more than is necessary for me. What more can I ask? Only that you continue to raise your grandchildren to keep Torah and *mitzvos*, so that Hashem will reckon everything you have done for the good. He will regard it as though you brought up your own children to observe Torah and *mitzvos*.

Ima: You said that everything in Heaven is dynamic and subject to change. Has your situation changed in Heaven? Will we still have to part soon?

Galia: Ima, everything is dynamic. But in my case there are things which are already fully decided. I was given an extension in order to prepare you psychologically and and to remain while you continued working on another book about me. Now my *tikun* has come to an end in the best possible manner. I thank Hashem for all the *zechus* which has fallen to our lot. But now that extension is also coming to its end, and this is a great relief for my soul. My soul is happy and delighted that soon the suffering and pain of its existence in this world will be over.

✢ Parting Message To Her Father

Galia: Ima, tell my dear dad that I love him very much. He took care of me a great deal when I was a little child and loved me a lot. But he also chose to part with me a long time ago. Even though I am still here, he parted with me a long time ago.

Ima, I am not angry with him. I fully understand his difficulty. He is a large part of my suffering in this world, and that too is part of my *tikun*. But what can I do? The situation seems helpless. All I can do is to cry inside the hidden parts of my heart and pray that the situation will somehow change.

❧ *Parting Message To Her Brothers*

Galia: Ima, tell my dear brothers that I love them and always loved them. Even if they were so embarrassed over the way I am. But I understand they are not to be blamed, because how can you be proud of a sister like me?

Ima, tell them that now they can be proud of me, of their sister, because they can read about me and get to know their true Galia who loves them so much for the first time. And they can tell their friends about me and be proud of this sister of theirs. Not every boy has the privilege of being brother to a girl like me who got her mother to do *teshuva*. Ask them how many girls, little girls of my age, got a grown up mother like you to do *teshuva*.

❧ *A Message To Those Who Sent Us Letters*

Ima: Galia, do you have a message for all those who responded to the (first) book about you and all the thanks, the *brachos* and love which people sent you?

Galia: Dear Ima, pass on to each one of them one common message. I am completely delighted to see that the inner being of the beloved, holy Jewish people is all love for one's fellow.

To all those wonderful people who wrote letters, I am sorry that it is technically impossible for me to reply personally to everyone who contacted me. People, in all their enormous love for me, forget that in fact I do not have the physical means to understand or to write. All communication is with the soul. Let it be regarded as though they have received an answer. All the letters are very beautiful and really touching. I love you all. *Baruch Hashem* that I had the *zechus* to win the love of the Jewish People. My dear Ima, I feel the true and authentic love of all who write letters inquiring how I am. This provides me the *shefa* of the highest *shefas*. Love melts barriers, breaks borders, creates reciprocity and the happiness of the lover and the beloved. It is impossible to live without love. Lack of love causes depletion of personality, terrible sadness, and illness. Love gives enormous vitality and motivates us to act, rejoice, create, and do things for His Name in love. I pray that *HaKadosh Baruch Hu* will send every Jew blessing and success. May they merit seeing the arrival of *Mashiach tzidkainu* quickly without pain, without torment and suffering, and may they have the *zechus* to love and be loved.

✢ *Last Words*

Ima: I am sorry that in my terrible insensitivity, at first I thought that your birth was a blow that had come to ruin my life. It's clear to me now that you are the most wonderful gift that a mother can hope for. Thanks and praise to *HaKadosh Baruch Hu* who gave you to me, my beloved Galia.

Galia: A man can never know what he'll get to do in life. All the opportunities are open. And we are a good example of that.

Ima: I want you to know, Galia, that wherever you are and any time, you should know that I love you very much. Always. Forever. For eternity. Thank you very much for all the patience you had for me in all the messages and all the wonderful communication we had. Thank you very much for all the fantastic messages you passed on to me and the Jewish people. I am very sorry if I caused you any pain with all my questions.

Galia: Ima, I want to tell you that you are all my love in this world, the happiness which lit up my whole life here. You are my beloved *tzadekes*. You are the only one who is mine in our world, this world of falsity. You are the only true love I had all my life. I am unable to thank you for all you did for me, for all the *mitzvos* with which you adorned my soul and enabled me to rise very high in the high worlds.

My dear Ima, *b'ezras Hashem*, we will meet after one hundred and twenty years in the next world, and you will see what a wonderful *zechus* you and I have because of you. The two of us will be there together all the time and never part again forever. Our parting is temporary, only in this material world. We will never separate spiritually. We are linked by iron cables, forever.

My beloved Ima, I am happy and delighted to leave behind all this terrible suffering and sadness and loneliness which was my lot all my life in this world. You saved me with your love for me and all your attention. You gave me an opening of light, a window which the sun breaks through and sends me such smiling and caressing rays. You are my faithful support who has never abandoned me for a moment. Your love lifts up my being and my spirit, and gives me fantastic strengths. From time to time, a loving and warming ray of sun breaks through the black and heavy clouds gathered over my sky. My dear mother, you are the one who is my ray of sun which breaks through and warms and uplifts my whole being and spirit.

Ima, don't worry. I'll never leave you. I am only leaving my tired and worn down body which carried me with such great difficulty all my days. My soul never leaves you even for a moment. I am with you. I am yours and I am beside you. We are together spiritually all the time.

Ima: My beloved Galia, what's your opinion? Maybe I'll commission a *sefer Torah* to be written in honor of *HaKadosh Baruch Hu* and the Jewish people. Could that *sefer Torah* help to change you into a normal girl?

Galia: Stop deceiving yourself all the time. Even if you write a *sefer Torah*, which is a fantastic *mitzva*, it won't turn me into a normal child. Every soul has to execute the *tikun* imposed upon it in this world. My *tikun* has ended. So why should I stay here in this suffering when such happy worlds await me in Heaven? Ima, If you could heap up in a pile all the happiness of everyone in this world from the beginning of history until today, it would look like a tiny pile in comparison with one minute of the pleasure awaiting me in the high worlds. I hope I have succeeded in depicting my thoughts.

I thank and praise the King of the World for the *zechus* which I merited in succeeding in my mission and the *zechus* I was given of guiding you and communicating with you for the sake of my beloved Jewish people. Goodbye, my beloved mother, blessed unto Hashem, the Maker of Heaven and earth.

Your Galia who loves you.

Chapter Thirteen:
Ends and Beginnings,
The Conversations Continue

Chapter Thirteen

❧ Geula and Teshuva

You don't have to wait until Rosh Hashanah and Yom Kippur to do *teshuva*. A man can do *teshuva* every day of the year. *Tzadikim* do *teshuva* every night before they go to sleep. Even if a man does *teshuva* in his last dying hour, it is accepted.

There are three principles of *teshuva*: regret, confession and reform.

Regret means regretting what you did.

Confession means confessing to Hashem what you did.

Reform means undertaking to desist from the particular sin, not to act sinfully, and to be sure not to repeat the mistakes of the past.

Teshuva is a fantastic present given to us by Hashem. Heaven regards the one who has done *teshuva* as one who has gone to Jerusalem and rebuilt the *Beis Hamikdash*.

Nothing stops a person from doing *teshuva* if he wants to. *Teshuva* and *ma'asim tovim* are like a shield that protects a person from disasters.

⌇⌇⌇⌇

Ima: Galia, you say that the way Hashem runs the world is starting to be revealed. That is very exciting! Is the truth starting to be revealed? Hashem doesn't hide His face from us anymore?

Galia: Correct, Ima. What is occuring in our generation is very exciting. If only everyone would open his eyes to see this happiness which is coming down to the world, that Hashem loves us so much and is starting a new form of divine conduct with us — a *gilui panim* — a revealed face. In recent times, his control has been unapparent, but His control is now starting to become unveiled. My dear Ima, I am happy to tell you that the era of *hester panim* is finally passing from the world.

For those who keep Torah and *mitzvos, gilui panim* is wonderful. However, with the revelation of the rulership of Hashem in the world, those who do not fulfill Torah and *mitzvos* will have to be punished with even greater severity than in the era of the periods of *hester panim*. The judgment is perfect justice and there is no leniency.

We have to open our eyes and see the truth staring at us and not be like the ostrich which hides its head in the sand and doesn't see anything. We are obligated to open our eyes and see the truth which is starting to come down to us from Heaven, from the world of truth, to light up our oppressive darkness. Only Torah can light it up. Hashem is lighting up the terrible darkness in front of us through the truth, which is carving itself right in the midst of all this darkness. Fortunate are we, those who are privileged to see the light — both those who see the truth directly and those who see this illuminated truth indirectly.

Ima: Galia, what you are saying is frightening. How will it all end up?

Galia: Dear Ima, I am not saying these things in order to frighten, but to open people's eyes. So many go blindly after money, cheating, and exploiting, with lack of humility and modesty, looking for glory and material wealth, which are of no use in the pure and holy world.

The religious also have to wake up and understand that they have no license to commit the sins they do, sometimes serious ones, both knowingly and in secret. Many religious people have to do *teshuva*. Everything is open and known to the Master of Everything. You have to open your eyes and remember that everything will be judged and the judgment will be fair. Only erasure of the accusations which you have accumulated can help. Everything is achieved through *mitzvos*. We have to do more *mitzvos* for our brothers who do not observe Torah and *mitzvos*. Everyone should undertake to do *mitzvos* to help other people and then it is likely that the *gezaira* will be annulled.

Now is a wonderful time for this. *HaKadosh Baruch Hu* is giving all of us the opportunity to return to Him with love, pleasantly and at our own pace. This period will change very soon and everything will change. Tell everyone that we must make good use of this time. It will be easier for the Jewish people to do *teshuva* quickly, pleasantly, and willingly, without suffering and pain.

Ima, people by themselves are determining what will happen to them. They will be the only ones to finalize it. The coming days are days of favor, and Heaven accepts all requests. We have to make the first step and Heaven will take over and provide us all the help necessary. Everything revolves around trust in *HaKadosh Baruch Hu Yisbarach*. It is a great pity to see that people are so closed, and just think about themselves. But there are those who think about the nation, and in their *zechus*, the *geula* will be hastened.

We are already beginning to see how the light is starting to come down to this world through the pure souls that have prepared themselves to receive it. Ima, you saw and heard recently that there are rabbis and people with *ruach hakodesh* — divine inspiration. In the days of *Mashiach*, that's what there will be. *Ruach hakodesh* will spread and people will rise very high in their spiritual levels.

Galia: All the quiet in the world today is the quiet before the great storm. It's like a volcano which gives off smoke all the time. But no one in the world, even the scientists, know when it will suddenly explode. There will be no prior signs. It will explode suddenly like an erupting volcano and the situation for the Jewish people will be very difficult, worse than it has ever been since the founding of the State. Since the State was founded, Heaven has judged us with more severity because the State did not opt for the laws of the Torah. The punishment will be extremely hard for all of us Jews.

Before Hashem metes out a punishment like this, He tries to wake up and warn his children in order to save as many of them as possible. We have to continue all the time without stopping, to bring every Jew closer and fight for his soul so it won't be lost to us. The collective soul of the Jewish nation will not include those who did not return to Hashem. They will be in a pathetic state because they will not be able to belong to the soul of the nation, and the soul of the nation will not be truly complete without them. There is a strong mutual link. A person who worries about the nation is in fact worrying about himself also, that he will be a whole within a whole.

I am not allowed to say anything more precise or clear. The main principle is: suddenly, a blow, the return to Torah, and then at last — *geula*. When the blows strike – you wake up. It's impossible to go on being indifferent when you get hit. May Hashem have mercy on us, Amen! The more people who do *teshuva*, the more the blows will soften. Every soul which returns to Hashem causes the blow to get a great deal weaker.

My soul cries over my precious people all the time and I never stop praying for them. Prayer is very important and helps, especially in these mixed up days in which we need such a huge amount of Heaven's mercy.

Don't worry, because Hashem is proving to us that He protects us and that our nation will never be exterminated. Hashem treats us with and unlimited patience and great love that only such a loving father could have towards his misbehaved children. Those who have the *zechus* and spread Torah are in fact the protection for those who do not observe Torah and *mitzvos*. We constantly have to make sure that the Jewish people have many *zechuyos* in order to assure that a situation does not develop in which *chas vechalila,* the *zechuyos* will be less than the *chovos* – the demerits. Every individual in the Jewish nation must observe *mitzvos* and get others to observe *mitzvos* so as to increase the *zechuyos* of the Jewish nation, because we can never know what the current balance is. We always have to make the assumption that it's close to being even, but that there is still a danger of a *chova* — a debit balance, meaning a risk of Divine punishment. Therefore, we must always strive to bring the scales down on the credit side, because that's the only way we'll be saved from all the calamities which take place in the world.

Hashem loves us, His dear children, and wants to redeem us quickly, and we are in fact moving in the right direction. Unfortunately, *ba'alei teshuva* are still the smallest section of the whole people as such. The trend is wonderful, but the pace is still not fast enough, not forceful enough.

Anyone who devotes all of his energies to spreading Torah can arouse masses of people. Anyone who projects all his love to *HaKadosh Baruch Hu*, and his unceasing devotion, can help bring about a mass revival. Anyone with the spiritual and psychological capabilities, with the knowledge and the intelligence to organize and prepare material and persuasive talks, must go out to the public today and talk to the masses. This is the duty of the hour. All of us have to work hard for mass salvation, and Heaven will very severely judge anyone who can do this and doesn't. It's a special time now in which you still can save many Jewish souls from destruction.

Ima, Torah classes strengthening the people throughout the country and precious religious radio stations stir up joy, delight, happiness, and wonder in Heaven. They succeed in bringing masses of Jewish people closer to *HaKadosh Baruch Hu,* to Torah and *mitzvos* during such a critical period for our dear people. They should carry on in whatever way they can to inspire the masses. All those who spread Torah will obtain great things and salvation and protection. They cannot fathom how much Hashem loves them, or how great their reward will be. It is beyond all calculation and measure.

Ima, it's a time of crisis. We have to bring every precious Jew back to our Father in Heaven. The time is almost up. The sand in the hourglass has almost run out. Everything will soon change and then the *geula* will come. We will all feel like dreamers. Everything will depend on us, whether the *geula* will come easily, calmly, and gently or whether it will come the hard way.

Galia: We are in a very significant time for us; the *geula* is to arrive shortly. Those who do *teshuva* will be saved. The hard work of all those who spread Torah saves large numbers of people from going to ruin. My dear Ima, continue with your work with all your strength. It's a matter of saving lives. Strengthening people today is their rescue. In the era of the *Mashiach*, the gates of repentance are locked.

Ima: When will we be redeemed?

Galia: Ima, the *geula* has a defined date, very soon. Nobody knows the date. Only Heaven knows. Mankind does not know. Hashem pities his Jewish people and wants to redeem us already. How quickly it happens depends on us very much.

☙☙☙

Ima: There are people who give dates for the *geula*. What is the basis of their predictions?

Galia: Ima, they can say whatever they want. Only *HaKadosh Baruch Hu*, King of the World, decides what will be and when it will be, and nobody else. Nobody knows what *HaKadosh Baruch Hu* decides.

We are in one of the most likely times for the *geula*, more so than through all the generations and *b'ezras Hashem* very soon, we'll be worthy of greeting *Mashiach*. It's all very imminent. You cannot see what is happening beyond the material plane. I, the soul, see everything, and it's heartening to see all the mighty preparations in Heaven in anticipation of the *geula* of the Jewish people. My dear Ima, everything is moving and surging. Everything is preparing for the *geula*. Just as everything is already prepared for the *Shabbos* before it arrives — the candles, the food, the home, so too we are in the last few minutes left before lighting the *Shabbos* candles and the start of *Shabbos*. Heaven wants to redeem us. All of the gates of Heaven are open. We just have to put in a tremendous effort to this end to ensure that we can be part of it.

The Jewish nation has returned to its country, but even so, not everyone has returned to our Father in Heaven. It is impossible to make a division. We also have to return quickly to our loving Father, the King of the World. The Holy Land does not tolerate any *tum'ah*. The reestablishment of the true Israel can be based only on the Torah, the fear of G-d, purity of *midos*, love of one's fellow, brotherhood, peace and friendship among ourselves and between ourselves and our Father in Heaven.

Man has a fantastic power of influence. He has the power to change a great deal in all the worlds and his *ma'asim tovim* can bring the *geula* very near. The time has almost run out. There are only a few odd grains of sand left in the giant hour glass set in motion after the destruction of the second Temple. When the last grain of sand falls, there will be massive revelations and the *geula* of the Jewish nation will start.

Ima, we can speed up the last few grains of sand left in the hourglass of the world. We can speed them up so that they fall faster. Every single *mitzva* which the Jewish person undertakes speeds up the redemption processes and oils the cogs of the world and enables them to work as efficiently, correctly, and well as possible. Only the *mitzvos* of the precious Jewish people speed up and bring the *geula* nearer.

Everything is going to change so soon. Evil and the *yetzer hora* will disappear from the world very soon. The living, the vegetable, and the inanimate will change beyond recognition. Everything will find its wonderful and complete rectification in accordance with the planned goal of the world at the time of its creation. *Bracha* will enter the world and it will perfectly fulfill the purpose which Hashem gave it, to create growth, to build on the lines of truth, tranquility and peace. Inanimate matter also has high spiritual roots. The whole of this world is linked to high spiritual roots. There isn't one tiny thing detached from spirituality.

If people were to rise above themselves and free themselves from the ropes of our so-called enlightened science, they would be able to see the spiritual source of the whole creation.

Mashiach will be revealed *b'ezras* Hashem very soon and bring with him relief for all the pains of this sick and suffering world. All the hosts of Heaven are already prepared for the *geula* of the Jewish people. If only our minds were able to understand how much the whole Jewish people, every man and woman, is loved in Heaven. How we fail to understand our obligations, which were only made for our own good. With them, we can receive everything in the spiritual worlds with the great feeling that we strove, worked, and struggled to achieve them.

Very hard times are expected soon. That will change the closed thinking of many people. The suffering which will be in the world will purify those who are left, those whose many *klippos* have not been removed from them. The *tzadikim* who, through their doing *teshuva* and the effort they have put in spreading Torah, have already purified themselves and have gotten rid of many *klippos,* will hardly suffer from the pain and suffering that will come down to this world. Very soon the eyes of many, that have been closed until now, will open wide.

The end of the exile has come. The time for the *geula* has almost arrived and the destiny of the Jewish people is to do *teshuva*. We are witnesses to the fact that masses are doing *teshuva*. The flow will increase until all the Jews will be, *b'ezras Hashem*, a light for the nations, and they will believe in the Torah and fulfill the *mitzvos* of *Hashem Yisbarach*.

❧❧❧

Ima: My dear Galia, how are you feeling today?

Galia: *Baruch Hashem*, Ima. There are, *baruch Hashem*, campaigners getting the public to do *teshuva*. In Heaven, they are happy and Heaven helps each one of them, and each of them feels the help he gets from Heaven through the Torah that he explains in the classes that he gives to the public.

Regretfully, many of them have forgotten that people take to Torah in response to pleasant and respectful methods of persuasion. The main *teshuva* is in the inner person and the consummation of the inner person. That's the right way, and that's the truth and there is nothing else.

Dear Ima, there is a spark in every Jew, and the proof is that in difficult times, everyone wants to find out how to pray, and reads *Tehillim,* and has complete faith that Hashem will save him. Today, the hardest work is to preserve what exists and to continue to draw the new people who join the *teshuva* movement close. If we don't operate with pleasant methods, such as modesty and humility, we will lose the spirit that inspires the doing of *teshuva*. We will lose faith and trust in Hashem and many will find their path by returning to the non-religious life, *chalila*. We have to light up the person whose spark is already warm enough. The flame will burn at once and we'll stoke the coals. Everything must be done through pleasantness and courtesy, without compulsion.

B'ezras Hashem, we will all become pleasantly and mercifully inspired to go back to our Father in Heaven who loves us so much. We have to learn *midos tovos,* which will help us distinguish between the *yetzer hora* and the *yetzer hatov.* We must evade the *yetzer hora.* This is a major portion of our *tikun.* It is forbidden for us to lose hope. The person who works on his *midos* constantly goes through ups and downs and sometimes even extreme ups and downs. You have to watch out carefully and not get disheartened.

❧❧❧

Ima: Do you have anything else to write?

Galia: Dear Ima, mighty and wonderful revelations await us so soon. You have to be very careful of people who define themselves as messiahs.

❧❧❧

Soon there will be confusion. We, the Jewish people, are under an obligation to accept the pronouncements of the Torah leaders. *HaKadosh Baruch Hu* supervises them and directs them how to guide his precious children. At the time of the revelation of the *Mashiach*, the number of people who have risen to a high spiritual level will increase, and people will see and feel things such as there never were in all the generations. High spiritual realities that until now were the spheres only of some individuals will be shown to the public, who shall emerge as worthy of selection and worthy of the selections which shall follow.

As I have already told you, Ima, there will be selections all the time, and very soon there will be a massive selection and after it, slightly smaller selection processes. All these involved processes are expected to start soon. Fortunate are those who go the way of Hashem, who runs His world with love, understanding, and perfect justice. He gives no one in His world any preferential treatment. We have to look and think and then we will see how much *HaKadosh Baruch Hu* loves us, His beloved sons and His beloved daughters, and pities us and protects us from everything. We just have to open our eyes to look and see.

❧❧❧

Ima: After the exodus, why did the Jewish people want to go back to Egypt if it was so terrible for them there, and especially after they saw so many miracles and wonders?

Galia: Dear Ima, if you study the matter well, you'll see that the *erev rav* who joined the Jews were responsible for all the troubles and the sin of the Golden Calf. Today, too, a sizable part of the Jewish people are the *erev rav,* who try every way possible to cause troubles for the Jews and try to create a situation in which the nation will cease to survive, *chalila.* They will be the first to be harmed in the first selection. This can only warn us today and serve as an open, serious warning to all those who already know the truth, that they have to behave with extreme caution and trust Hashem and fulfill His *mitzvos.* Otherwise they will be punished more severely than all those who have still not discovered the truth.

Ima: Galia, when the Jews left Egypt, they left bondage for eternal freedom. They saw miracles and wonders. But how did they feel about having to start all over again, to wander in the desert for so many years without a roof and with all the difficulties that they entailed?

Galia: They were happy to be released from the wickedness of the Egyptians who subjected them to hard slave labor and were extremely cruel to them. Even the terrible desert was *Gan Eden* compared to Egyptian slavery. They had the *zechus* of seeing the mighty revelations, which we too, *b'ezras Hashem,* shall see in the not-too-distant future! As I have told you, we are the generation of the *geula.* And the truth is beginning to be revealed in our generation.

Your communicating with me is also one of the truths that are coming down into the world and being revealed. Now additional truths will be revealed all the time, and even more light will come down. It is impossible to bring down all the *shefa* of light at one time. People are not set up to receive a *shefa* of light all at once. Even the little truths and the small light that are starting to come down are hard for people to digest and understand. Hashem in His mercy and His enormous love for the Jews is sending the light and the *shefa elyon* to this world very slowly and gradually. Each time, a little *shefa* of light comes down until the complete truth will be revealed. We can now see a little of the truth which is penetrating the slits in the world's screen.

People are more aware of all that is happening in such areas as clinical death, *gilgulim* of souls, the Torah codes, and communication with the soul of the person with brain-damage. These are things which clearly show us about life after death and reveal the reality of this world as a place of temporariness and passing.

Galia: I am happy that Hashem opens our eyes and lets us see the truth, which at the moment is pouring down on the world. Fortunate are those who have the *zechus* to see this shining truth. Most people still don't. They have not pre-pared themselves to receive the light which is coming down to the world. Those who work on themselves can see a lit-tle of it because the light can penetrate clean and trans-parent containers. The closed containers (people who have not opened themselves to Torah and *mitzvos*) swallow the light and don't let it pass outwards. These closed contain-ers don't feel and don't see this light. Very soon this light will flood our world and no one will be able to be mistaken about it. The light will be genuinely perceptible. You will see it with your eyes.

Ima: What are you referring to? Are there going to be miracles?

Galia: Ima, there will be amazing revelations which the hu-man eye has never seen, and fortunate are those who will have the *zechus* to see them. To our great sorrow, it seems that most people won't. But as I told you, there are changes all the time. Everything is dynamic and changes, and if only as many precious Jews as possible will go back quickly to our Father in Heaven, then they will get to see the miracles and wonders which await us soon.

⮌⮌⮌

Galia: The salvation of the Jews will happen soon. The *geula* of the Jewish nation is near. Ima, the end is getting very near. It's already here at the entrance. Our generation will *b'ezras Hashem* have the *zechus* to see mighty events and the fulfillment of the prophecies. We all have to become pure quickly. Only purification can enable us to receive the light which is so mighty and wonderful. All the dirty receptacles will explode. When the big light comes, they will explode because they won't be able to bear it. They are unsuited for this. Only clean receptacles will be able to receive it and disperse it. The light can only be placed in shiny, gleaming receptacles which it can pass through, and not in dirty receptacles which stop it.

⮌⮌⮌

Galia: My brothers and sisters, don't sleep. Get up. Wake up. See the truth. All those who do *teshuva* prevent disaster, but that too is not enough. People don't understand the simple axiom that there is a Creator. There is accountability and there is a Judge. The end is drawing close fast, and it's possible that there may not be enough time to do teshuva.

Jews of the world, wake up! There's no time to wait. Time's up. Love your fellow as yourself. I am the Lord your God who took you out of Egypt. That's the message.

⮌⮌⮌

❧ Mysticism And Seances

Galia: Recently the phenomenon of mysticism has spread a great deal in addition to the spread of studying non-Jewish doctrines that are linked to impurity which mix in the Heavenly Hosts and turn everything upside down.

Those who dabble, so to speak, in mysticism and try to communicate with spirits must understand that *Kabala* is not street-type mysticism and that a Jew is not allowed to call up spirits. Every attempt by a person who does not keep Torah and *mitzvos* and doesn't keep *Shabbos* and put on *tefillin* and keep an extra holiness to communicate with spirits results in communicating with the forces of impurity. He becomes contaminated by them and they confuse his mind, and he ends up hurt both physically and spiritually.

It is thoroughly unacceptable for teenagers try to talk to dead relatives by sitting together in some impure spot, indecently dressed, and think that they are talking with their dead relatives when in fact they are talking to demons. Heaven would certainly not give permission to the youths to talk to a holy soul through a board and a cup in the air raid shelters, where in all probability there is no *kedusha* and there's not even a *mezuza*.

Only *tum'ah*, for which such conditions are extremely conducive, responds to teenagers and adults who try to communicate with worlds of holiness. Doing this puts them and their families in danger. *Tum'ah* will not give away anything for nothing and it has the permission of Heaven to harm anyone who messes with it. They damage the minds, the spirits, and the souls of the people conducting the seance or any practice of *tum'ah*. You have to explain to the public that the whole business of the seance is rooted in *tum'ah*. It's a way for external forces to cling to a person. You should have nothing to do with these things at all. You can get irreparably damaged physically and mentally.

Ima, it's very important that they know how to distinguish between *tum'ah* and the messages that pass through my soul in holiness and purity, with the body serving merely as a technical instrument. You have to make a complete distinction between holiness and *tum'ah*, between black and white and between forbidden and permitted. There's no chance of getting accurate answers and information from a source which is entirely *tum'ah*. It's like a dream which comes through a demon. It has a little truth in it and all the rest is lies, because they were created for this purpose, to confuse people, and especially Jews, who are misled into following *tum'ah*. You have to warn Jews who fear for their fate and that of their children and their families, that not only is there nothing in all this but anyone who makes use of the forces of *tum'ah* for any reason whatsoever causes himself to be uprooted from the world. That includes all those who meddle in "improving luck and fortune."

ᗰᗰᗰ

✢✤ *Reading Cards And Magic*

Ima: Should we include a section on magic in the book?

Galia: Definitely. It's very important that people know that Heaven tells people that it is forbidden to consult all those sorcerers and dangerous people. You have to tell the holy and precious Jewish people to stop taking advice and receiving or buying amulets and charms from people belonging to other religions and idolatry. All this reading of cards and coffee grinds, and all this massive flocking today to ask the advice of *tum'ah,* and going to all kinds of Arab sheiks who dabble in *tum'ah,* has to stop. All the blue eyes that are manufactured by Muslims in Turkey and all the various types of crimson threads are considered idolatry and conspiracy and magic.

They have to stop all this running after *tum'ah* at once which only strengthens the forces of *tum'ah* and in the end causes serious and indescribable and inestimable damage to all those who turn to this nonsense.

You have to make the public aware of it and warn them and keep them far from women who practice card-reading, who are from the primal sources of the *sitra achra*. All the images printed on cards are in fact from the images of the lower crowns [*Kabala*. A reference to an element of the dark forces, which parallel the high forces] from whom those women get their information. Just as there's no such thing as a kosher pig, so there's nothing holy about those cards. You cannot get correct answers from a source which is wholly *tum'ah*. There is a concept which makes Heaven very angry and that is "*Kabalistic* tarot cards" which is a "kosher pig". There's no such thing. It's sorcery.

It's forbidden to practice sorcery. All these are disgusting things and evil sorcery and the burning of incense to idols. Nothing good comes out of this. On the contrary, it damages the soul of masses of Jews and all kinds of ignorant people. Above all, you've got to be careful of women who communicate with angels. If Heaven gave its permission, the angel would appear to one of the holy *Rabbanim-mekubalim* who works in holiness and purity for free, without payment, not to a woman whose only object is money and praise. She talks to demons and says she is communicating with angels. My dear Ima, it makes Heaven very angry.

❧❧❧

❧ Practical Kabala and Amulets

Ima: What's your opinion of all those who dabble in practical *Kabala* and amulets?

Galia: Today, unfortunately, there are various rabbis who practice, so to speak, practical *Kabala,* whose sole object is the making of money. They do not have any notion or even half a notion of practical *Kabala.* They're nothing but sorcerers dabbling in things with no permission from Heaven. They are actually causing harm with a combination of *tum'ah* and *kedusha* between which they do not know how to differentiate.

The source of this [dabbling in *Kabala*] is in a large number of books on practical *Kabala* on the market, new books which come out every day by people whose object is money and fame, and which are sold to anyone who pays.

It's completely unacceptable to photocopy an amulet which has holy names on it or to burn an amulet which has the name of *Hashem Yisbarach* on it.

You shouldn't melt lead over someone's head, claiming that it gets rid of the evil eye. *Tefillin, tallis,* Torah and *mitzvos* are the real protection against all these things. Not lead which belongs to the externals. There are religious people who do this and they don't know that they are dealing with *tum'ah.*

The books I mentioned contain false amulet texts and amulet texts written by gentiles a long time ago. As an outcome of the exile, books which were not really dealing with true Jewish *kabala* became intermingled with our literature. There's also a lot of confusion in religious works which were originally written by *tzadikim.* But with the decline of the generations, Heaven brought it about that there be confusion with the holy names so that people who dabble in this for prestige and pride, and act not for the sake of Heaven, will not be able to use them successfully. Masses of Jews learned how to dabble in *tum'ah* during the exile, especially among the Muslims in their various countries. Without knowing what the sources are, they mixed *kedusha* and *tum'ah* together without realizing. This confusion is found today in loads of books. Heaven opens the eyes of a few special people and helps them to separate the good from the bad.

Ima, a lot of books on practical *Kabala* are endorsed by known rabbis who, in some cases, were deceived. The entire text was not shown to the rabbis with all the terrible things that were written in it. They signed letters of approval, not always being to blame, as though the books were fit. The *Shechina* screams out and cries over the pain these "authors" cause themselves and Hashem.

Dear Ima, you should be extremely careful of all kinds of forged and photocopied amulets sold today by the thousands everywhere, including at the tombs of *tzadikim*. Not only are they invalid and don't help at all, but they also harm the owner. They were only written for materialistic reasons and not for the sake of Heaven, in holiness and purity.

❧ *Arab Sheiks and Fortune Tellers*

Ima: I heard about people who consult Arab sheiks. What do you say about that?

Galia: Ima, it hurts me a lot. I see how those Jews who go to ask the advice of the forces of evil are harmed. Tell everyone not to go to any kind of Arab sheik; they give answers to questions by means of the oaths of demons or evil spirits. Many Jews have been more harmed than helped by this. That is the method of the *sitra achra*. At first they give you the feeling as though the sheik helps more than all the rabbis whom the Jew has gone to. But after a short time, they cause damage.

Don't go to all kinds of Arabs who try to mislead the Jewish public and to all kinds of women fortune tellers who get the information they pass on in return for being well rewarded by the *sitra achra*. Understand that it is important to the *sitra achra* to attract Jews because then they can be mislead with folly, evilness of the spirit and lies. Additionally, it can also draw from the forces of holiness.

❧ *The Crimson Thread*

Ima: Can you give us a little more information about the crimson thread?

Galia: Ima, the crimson thread is something which has spread recently. Not only is it an act of the Emori -idolatry in biblical Israel, it is expressly forbidden by the Torah and has no blessing and no holiness. It's just a means of making money by charging 5,000 shekels for a ball of thread which costs 20 shekels, and then telling people that it's a *mitzva,* and that it's for charity. Dear Ima, you have to make it clear that someone who is ill and lying and on his deathbed suffers more because of that thread. It adds strength to the *sitra achra*. And the crimson thread comes from the side of the judgments which rule through the color of judgment, red, which they have on. One should not allow any string to be tied on the hand. There is no blessing in this!

❧ *The Keys To Better Luck*

Ima: Are those people who hand out keys and locks to open up your luck also part of all what you're saying?

Galia: Dear Ima, the lock which is supposed to open up the luck of singles has an element of sorcery. It doesn't help to find a partner in the slightest. That is something that is predetermined before a person is even born. Charms like these are mentioned in books about *Kabala* and charms. I've already explained to you that there are many books with mistakes and sections copied from non-Jewish publications and their practices. That is the result of Jews living among gentiles. There are rabbis who are misled by the mistakes in these books and instead of checking up, they make a mistake and mislead loads of others without them knowing. My beloved Jewish people has to understand that only the holy Torah and complete and absolute faith in *HaKadosh Baruch Hu* will make us successful and cancel all kinds of disasters and hard *gezairos*. That way, we will be saved from all our visible and invisible enemies and from all kinds of *kitrugim*.

～～～

❧ *The Evil Eye*

Ima: Galia, do thought and words have a power to change things?

Galia: Sure. Jealousy and hate in the heart have a negative power which can cause a person to feel bad. Jealousy and hate are the evil eye. But if a person is protected by *maasim tovim*, simple faith and Torah study, there is no danger.

The evil eye is the force a person has in his eyes to harm others because he is jealous of them and his eye is resentful. He can't bear someone else's good fortune. So he harms them even without realizing it and projects poison to them and it harms their health. The evil eye has very destructive power. Ima, tell everyone to work on this trait and they themselves should develop a good eye.

Ima: How do you take care not to be harmed by the evil eye?

Galia: A person must observe Torah and *mitzvos*. Then he is less vulnerable than others who don't observe Torah and *mitzvos*. But what helps the most is helping others, which really protects a person from the evil eye.

❧ *Television*

Galia: Ima, television is a very big *tum'a*. Tell everyone to get this *tum'a* out from their homes as soon as possible. Watching so much rubbish and sexual indecency causes the soul great damage.

Instead of studying Torah or performing *mitzvos*, people waste their lives passively watching something which is of no benefit and no purpose at all. Television is *tum'a*.

❧ *Abortions*

Ima: When does the soul enter the body? Is it before birth?

Galia: Before. The moment the child is formed.

Ima: So those who perform abortions kill someone who has a soul?

Galia: Yes. Abortion is terrible suffering for the soul of the child.

Ima: A woman who performs an artificial miscarriage — she's a murderess?

Galia: It depends. You have to ask a rabbi in every case.

Ima: If the rabbi tells her that it is forbidden to have an abortion, and she has one, is she a murderess?

Galia: She's worse than that. She rebels against Hashem.

Ima: Can a murderer also do *teshuva* and is his *teshuva* accepted by Heaven?

Galia: A true *teshuva* ... certainly.

༄༄༄

๑๛ *Overeating*

Ima: Galia, can you advise as to how to overcome craving food?

Galia: Dear Ima, *baruch Hashem* that you overcame worse inclinations than that. And with the help of Hashem, you will overcome that too. Part of your self-development work, and everyone's, is to overcome base desires and tendencies which dominate us. Like every evil, it's all the urging of the *yaitzer hara,* who gives a person evil advice. You have to control it. Every crude desire you don't get the better of causes great damage, both spiritual and physical. The destruction is apparent.

After one hundred and twenty, when a man leaves his body and his soul goes up, nothing is hidden there. Everything is clear. All the damage he caused. And he is extremely pained by this. Death is hard for those with strong, crude desires. After death, a lot of suffering awaits the person who didn't succeed in subduing crude desires while he was in his body. It finally purifies and cleans the soul of all the *tum'a* and the *yaitzer hara* which clung to it.

༄༄༄

๑๛ *Visits To The Sick*

Galia: Visiting the sick is a *mitzva* of the Torah. You have to visit the sick. It helps them and encourages them. It's very important to read *Tehillim* for them so as to increase their *zechus* in Heaven. And if the *kitrug* is removed from them due to the prayer, they'll get well. Visiting the sick is a very deep matter and a big *tikun* both for the sick person and the visitor.

～～～

❧ *Independence Day*

Galia: Ima, this Independence Day is a bitter day for us, the Jewish people, because since our independence, we have been judged more severely over every single thing. The State did not choose to follow the laws of Torah and this is a big problem that makes difficulties for the whole Jewish people.

～～～

❧ *Religious Radio Stations*

Ima: Do the Torah talks and discussions, which you hear from time to time, in class on the radio, on the religious channels, do good for you and the other children in the class?

Galia: I want to tell you that every soul loves to hear Torah talks and discussions.

Ima: Do you like listening to songs?

Galia: Religious songs, yes. Ima, I want to tell you that all these religious radio stations are doing an enormous amount for the cause of Heaven.

Tell everyone that the time is very significant and great, and everyone has to do *teshuva* because there is no time and also there is no other way. It's impossible to keep going on the path of sin. There has to be a change. To go only the way of Hashem. There is no other way.

For us Jews in these difficult times, religious radio channels are like air for the soul. All these fine religious radio channels are succeeding in bringing masses of Jews to *HaKadosh Baruch Hu*. All those who support these religious radio channels are partners in these important *mitzvos* of bringing Jews to religion in this terribly fateful period for our precious people. They should carry on a full-scale operation in whatever way they can to wake up the masses. All their activity is blessed, precious, and desired by Heaven.

All those who spread Torah amoung the Jewish people will see great things, salvation and great, wonderful events. In Heaven, they cause joy, delight, happiness and admiration. They cannot imagine how much Hashem loves them. Their reward will be beyond all measure and calculation!

Dear Ima, lately the radio channels have suffered many disruptions – namely government interference. The forces of *tum'ah* are at war over their existence and we have to fight in order to lay down a path to the truth, purity and light which will break through and shine on us.

The radio is a mighty powerful tool which reaches the masses in their homes. The words of the holy Torah are able to get inside their homes without any effort. The religious radio channels, which are involved in holiness for the sake of Heaven, are magnificent. They must continue spreading Torah among the masses. Masses of Jews are coming back to our Father in Heaven because of the precious religious radio channels.

It's very important that these channels preserve purity of conduct, holiness and perfect faith. It's also important that the messages they put out on the radio and the relations between the staff members are decent. They should be extremely careful because these things are critical for the preservation of our souls.

Ima, Heaven will only help the person whose whole purpose is the cause of Heaven and who does everything honestly and with perfect decency. Those who do not do things according to the principles of the Torah are destined for a mighty fall. Only the religious channels which are honest, decent and clean will survive.

Religious stations are waging wars to the death with the forces of wickedness and *tum'ah* which make accusations all the time and try to cause disruption. Any wounded animal can illustrate how an angry creature fights furiously for its life and is unafraid of anything. It has already lost everything and its life has melted away forever in front of its own eyes. Similarly, the forces of *tum'ah* can see that they have lost the war. That is the reason that there is so much trouble and confusion in the whole Jewish nation. As the *geula* gets nearer, the confusion becomes deeper. This is the last stand of the forces of evil, which has lost the battle from the onset. That is the reason why they are fighting with such force. They continually try to cause ever greater damage rather than have anything to do with holiness.

Soon, many aspects of the media will change, and a very few number of legal licenses for a limited number of religious stations will be awarded. It all depends on the clean conduct of all those serving what is holy on the religious channels. Those who are unfit and put on a show as if they are fit are the rot inside the apple, and the rot is spreading. So you have to get rid of the rot first with a knife and stop the rot from spreading, and then the apple will be magnificently beautiful.

Photos

Galia playing with toys in her house

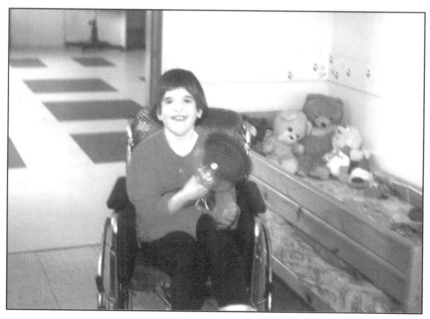

Galia in her dorm room

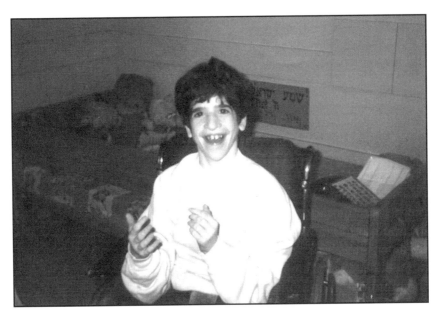

Galia in her dorm room

Ima and Galia

On Tuesday, 12/21/99, Ima appeared live on Channel 2,
on the Israeli prime-time show, Avraham and Yaakov,
in front of a million viewers.

Channel 2 Interview of Ima,
during which there was also
a short clip of a session with Galia.

Ima as a soldier
before being chozer b'teshuva

Ima after being chozer b'teshuva, speaking

Appendix

Websites and Information

WORTHWHILE WEB SITES

On Mysticism and Judaism

Aish Hatorah – http://aish.com/
Site in English offering a large collections of essays on life and religious topics from the Torah point of view.

Arachim – http://www.arachim.org.il
Site in Hebrew, offering a large collections of essays on life from the Torah point of view, and religious topics.

Bar Ilan University's parshat hashavua page —
http://www.biu.ac.il/JH/Eparasha/index.shtml
Site in English offering a variety of essays on present and previous parshiot.

Chabad —
English: http://www.chabad.org/
Hebrew — http://www.chabad.org.il
A well organized site offering a deluge of information about Torah and Chabad.

Efrat — http://www.efrat.org.il/
A Site in Hebrew and English about the Efrat organization and its activities to prevent abortion in Israel and help distressed pregnant women.

Ezra Lemarpe— http://ezra-lemarpe.bashan.co.il
Site in Hebrew, with some English information on the famous, independent, medical aid organization.

Hidabrut – http://www.hidabroot.org
Excellent site in Hebrew about the world from the Torah point of view.

KOSHERNET – http://site.safelines.net/
Filtered home page, well organized, offers a lot.

Manof – http://www.manof.org.il
Site in Hebrew and English, very professional, defining the position of Torah-life in modern Israeli society in a collection of articles; with link for viewers' contributions.

Moreshet — http://moreshet.co.il
Home page in Hebrew with a mosaic of links to news, informa-
tion, classifieds, events, advertising, etc. Notable graphic pres-
entation — respectful to the intelligence, pleasure to read, free
of all offensive content.

OU — http://www.ou.org
The OU organization's page in English, offering information
about OU and Judaism and articles. Excellent search engine
for Torah sites.

Rachliner Rebbe —
English site: http://www.rachlin.org.il/English/English.htm
Hebrew site — http://www.rachlin.org.il/index.htm
A very interesting site, offering the Rebbe's wisdom and advice
for a successful life.

Radio 10 – http://www.radio10.co.il/
A site mainly in Hebrew, but also in English and French, offer-
ing radio broadcasts, articles, events, information.

Radio 2000 — http://www.radio2000.co.il
A site mainly in Hebrew, but also in English, offering radio
broadcasts, articles, events, information.

Shema Yisrael — http://www.shemayisrael.com
A major site in English, offering information, articles, news,
services, study programs, etc. Important to visit.

Shofar — http://www.shofar.net/site/index.asp
Rav Amnon Yitzchak's site in Hebrew with some English, offer-
ing tape broadcasts, information, viewers contributions, forum.

STAM (site housed in Yahoo) —
http://www.geocities.com/MadisonAvenue/Suite/4069/1.html
All you need to know about the sefer Torah, tefillin and
mezuzah

Temple Institute — http://www.templeinstitute.org/main.html
An amazing site in English about the Temple Institute at 36
Misgav Ladach Street, Jewish Quarter, Old City, Jerusalem
97500, full of photos and articles about the Beis Hamikdash
(Temple) and information about the Institute.

Torah Codes — http://www.torahcodes.co.il
> *A Site in English. Doron Witztum's site on the amazing Torah codes phenomenon. Full scale academic study.*

Tzohar — http://www.tzohar.com/
> *A site in English and Hebrew on the activities of the Tzohar kiruv organization.*

On Facilitated Communication

Facilitated Communication Institute — http://soeweb.syr.edu/thefci/
> *An important site on facilitated communication by the Facilitated Communication Institute of Syracuse University, New York State, under the direction of world expert on FC, Prof. Douglas Biklen. Contains details of access to facilitated communication around the world and a very large collection of learned articles.*

Deal Communication Centre — www.vicnet.net.au/~dealccinc
> *A site of Rosemary Crossley's center for facilitated communication in Melbourne, Australia, containing information about the center and facilitated communication.*

Carol Lee Berger — soeweb.syr.edu/thefci/1-3ber.htm
> *Carol Lee Berger's contribution to the site of the Facilitated Communication Institute of Syracuse U.*

Israeli site on FC — FaclilitatedCommunication.f2s.com/
> *Photos and articles in English.*

More Material On Galia

Visit our web site in English and Hebrew: www.signsfromHeaven.com
Galia. Messages From Heaven, **a film on video with English subtitles**, featuring a talk by Shulamit Gad, the mother of Galia, a communication session with Galia, a demonstration of the authenticity of the messages, the peak-hour interview with Shulamit on Israeli TV.
Galia. Messages From Heaven, in Hebrew, the latest edition of the best-selling book in Israel.

Galia. Messages From Heaven, on CD, in Hebrew
Lecture tapes and pamphlets in Hebrew.

Galia Site information

Galia — http://www.signsfromHeaven.com/
A Site in Hebrew and English. Our own site on the communi-
cations with Galia. Links to excerpts from the books. Heavily
illustrated, including photos that do not appear in the books.

Kiruv Organizations

Contact these organizations for advice and information on seminars,
religious institutions, etc., both in Israel and the Diaspora.

Arachim (Israel) —Tel: 02-500-0220, 03-579-3035

Judaism From A Different Angle (Israel) — the organization of the
well known lecturer, Harav Noigerschall. Tel: 02-581-6573

Lev L'Achim (Israel) — Tel: 03-578-1782

National Center For Family Purity (Israel) — 28 Yisa Bracha Street,
Jerusalem. Tel: 02-582-0414

Shabbos With Rav Elbaz (Israel) — Spend *Shabbos* with Rav Elbaz
shlita in the Or Hachayim Yeshiva in Jerusalem. (For singles [men]
who have completed military service.) Tel: 02-500-0455

Selah (Israel) — Women's seminar for Jewish studies.
Tel: 03-618-3275

Shofar (Israel) — the organization of Harav Amnon Yitzchak, Bnei
Brak. Tel: 03-677-7779

Center For Jewish Information (Israel) — Tel: 02-581-1911

Tzohar (Israel) — Tel: 02-500-0807

Yeshivat Netivot Olam for Ba'alei Teshuva (Israel) — Aharaonvitz
(Hashomer) Street/corner Hashlosha Street, Bnei Brak.
Tel: 03-579-4210

FC Information

The Internet address of the institute is: www.soeweb.syr.edu/thefci.

It is important to note that there are hundreds of sites on FC, reporting on this astonishing method of communication, providing a great deal of updated information on the subject.

Through the Facilitated Communication Institute site (and others), you can obtain a catalogue and order a large variety of reading material and audio and video tapes pertaining to Facilitated Communication, as well as access a complete bibliography on the subject.

The Institute's telephone number is: 315-443-9657.

The address of the Institute is: The Facilitated Communication Institute, Syracuse University, 370 Huntington Hall, Syracuse, New York 13244-2340.

The institute regularly organizes lectures, committees, training, demonstrations and workshops throughout the U.S. and the world, especially in the framework of a large number of important organizations. Some of these include: The American Association of Psychiatry, The Handicapped Union, The American Association for Hearing, Speech and Language, The American Association For Mental Retardation, The World Institute For Special Education, Yokosoka, Japan, The World Committee For Technical Support For Parents, Washington DC, and The Society for Autism in America.

Bring our Jewish brothers and sisters to their Father in Heaven. Share in the *mitzva* of *zikuy harabim* — of bringing merit to the many. Distribute this book and the video with English subtitles to friends, family, and contacts.

For information on obtaining the above material and lectures, contact Israel Book Shop, 501 Prospect Street, Lakewood NJ 08701. Tel: (732) 901-3009, Fax: (732) 901-4012, email: isrbkshp@aol.com. Or email the author: shoulamitg@hotmail.com.

Glossary

Glossary

Adam Harishon lit. first man. Adam of the Genesis story.

After 120 in Jewish tradition, a euphemistic method of referring to a person's death. "When you're 120," i.e., *When you die* ...

Aishes chayil accomplished wife, i.e., a woman dedicated to a home of Torah. Also the text of the poem about the *aishes chayil* (*Proverbs* 31:10-31)

Aleihem hashalom of blessed memory, plural

Baalas teshuva feminine form of *baal tshuva*, a woman, formerly non-religious, who has become religious

Baba Sali popular name for Rabbi Yisrael Abuchatzeira, a great Torah personality who made a deep impression on the Israeli public from his arrival in 1964 to his death in 1984.

Bas kol Heavenly voice. In the Talmud, etc., the voice called out to individuals on special occasions. Galia stresses an aspect of it referred to in Zohar, a voice in Heaven that announces imminent world events.

Baruch Hashem Thank G-d

Beis Hamikdash the Temple

B'ezras Hashem with G-d's help

Bnei Yisrael the Jewish people

Bracha blessing

Chas v'chalila/Chas v'sholom G-d forbid

Chazal the Mishnaic and Talmudic sages

Cheder children's school

Chesed kindness

Chet ha-egel sin of the Golden Calf

Chova demerit; debt

Chovos plural of *chova*

Divrei Torah lit. words of Torah, i.e. Torah speeches, comments, etc., written or verbal

Erev Rav lit. great multitude. Historically, a group of Egyptians who joined the Jews in the Exodus from Egypt and acted as a fifth column, seeking to undermine the Jews' high spiritual goals. Figuratively, the *Erev Rav* is understood to be a perpetual element of the Jewish people until the Redemption and is, therefore, still active today.

Gan Eden Garden of Eden, Heaven

Gehinom Hell, purgatory

Geula the redemption. G-d will redeem the world from the forces of evil by bringing the Messiah.

Gezaira decree in Heaven, usually sent to punish through adversity, even catastrophe. (Gezaira tovah, on the other hand, means a good decree.)

Gezairos plural of *gezaira*

Gilgul incarnation. In general, part of the theory, popularized under the influence of the great seventeenth century kabalist, the Ari, that this world is a sphere of spiritual rectification (*tikun*). Rectification is achieved through ethical living and through suffering to atone for sins. A soul is sent to this world to achieve rectification. If it completes its life here and fails, it may be sent back to this world (*gilgul*) to strive again for rectification. It is accepted that nearly everyone today is a *gilgul*.

Gilgulim plural of *gilgul*

Hagaon the genius

Halacha Jewish law

Hashem lit. "the name." G-d

Hashem Yisbarach God, may He be blessed

Hakodosh Boruch Hu lit. the Holy One Blessed Be He. G-d

Ima mother; Mommy

Kabala Jewish mysticism

Kaddish mourner's prayer to help a dead soul

Kaddish d'rabanan similar to the regular *kaddish*, but including also a blessing for Torah scholars

Kedusha holiness; the forces of holiness

Kedusha ila'is high holiness

Kiruv lit. bringing close. Outreach. Activities — e.g., seminars, lectures, public meetings, talking to people in the street, special yeshivos, etc. — to influence the non-religious to become religious

Kitrug accusation, i.e., in Heaven. Man on earth is continually judged in Heaven. Misdeeds can provoke accusation which may lead to punishment. Kitrug can be directed at individuals, groups, nations, etc.

Kitrugim plural of *kitrug*

Klippa lit. shell. In *kabala*, evil forces with an encasing action, a heritage of the formation of the world. Galia uses the term to denote how sin can attract mystic forces of evil (the *klippa*) which proceed to consolidate a presence of destructive, evil influence. Through good deeds, one may remove the *klippa* (shell).

Klippos plural of *klippa*

Loshon hora lit. evil speech; speaking badly of people, considered a grave sin

Leilui nishmas lit. for the ascension of the soul. The fate of the soul in Heaven is re-evaluated from time to time, especially on the yahrzeit (anniversary of the death). If fortunate, a soul will rise a level. Good deeds in this world for the sake of the dead soul — *le-ilui nishmat* — can influence Heaven to grant the soul ascension.

Leilui nishmas hatzadik for the elevation of the soul of the *tzadik*

Ma'asim tovim good deeds

Mashchis lit. destroyer, a destructive angel

Mashiach the Messiah

Mashiach tzidkainu our righteous Messiah

Maseches Tractate; volume of Mishna or Talmud

Mazikim damaging spirits

Mekatraig a prosecutor in Heaven. See *kitrug.*

Melave malka a ritual meal held after *Shabbos* to accompany the Queen of *Shabbos* on her departure

Melitz yosher advocate in Heaven on behalf of an individual, the Jewish people, etc. A *melitz yosher* may be an angel or a departed *tzadik,* or any person with the *zechus* to act as a *melitz yosher.*

Melitzei yosher plural of *melitz yosher*

Metakayn rectify, set right

Mezakai harabim those who give merit to the masses. See *zikuy harabim*.

Mezakeh harabim verb form of *mezakai harabim*. Gives the masses merit. See *zikuy harabbim*.

Mida singular of *midos*.

Midos lit. measurements. Character traits. Judaism believes a person can use his will to convert his behavioral trends (*middos*) into consistent, virtuous, positive conduct.

Midos tovos good character traits

Mikva purification bath

Miruk lit. vigorous polishing, a process in Heaven to purify the soul

Mishna authoritative book of Jewish oral law

Mitzva G-d's commandment; meritorious deed

Mitzvos plural of *mitzva*

Modeh Ani prayer said on waking up in the morning

Mussar lit. admonition, i.e., inspiration to search one's soul and improve one's conduct

Neshama soul

Nitzotzos lit. sparks. In kabalistic theory, shards of light trapped in *klippos* (see *klippos*). A person's devotion to Hashem releases these sparks and moves the world forward to its restoration.

7 Noahide Laws The Torah is a doctrine for all man regardless of race, religion, or creed. Most of its laws or *mitzvos* are for Jews; however, it provides seven *mitzvos* for non-Jews: prohibition of idolatry; prohibition of blasphemy and cursing the name of G-d; prohibition of murder; prohibition of robbery and theft; prohibition of immorality and forbidden sexual relations; prohibition of removing and eating a limb from a live animal; requirement to establish a judicial system and courts of law to enforce the other six laws.

Or haganuz lit. hidden light. A light withdrawn from the world early in Creation and reserved for *tzadikim*.

Pargod screen cutting off Heaven from human view

Parsha weekly Torah reading

Parshios plural of *parsha*

Poskim religious legal authorities

Rabbanim plural of rabbi, a body of authoritative rabbis.

Rasha man who practices evil

Rashaim plural of *rasha*

Rav Rabbi

Sandak at a *bris mila*, person given the honor of holding the baby

Sefer book, as in *Sefer Torah* (Torah scroll)

Shabbos Sabbath

Shechina Divine Presence; G-d

Shefa lit. plenty. The force Heaven sends to this world which provides it with its material and spiritual supply.

Shefa elyon higher form of *shefa*

Shema (Yisrael) basic prayer affirming a Jew's faith in G-d recited twice a day. Sometimes recited before death.

Shiva seven days of mourning following burial of a close relative

Shlita acronym for "He shall live to a good old age"

Shoteh mentally incompetent; person lacking normal intelligence. According to Jewish law, a *shoteh* is exempt from all religious requirements.

Sitra achra lit. "the other side". Refers to forces of evil, i.e. Satan

Siyata d'shmaya the help of Heaven

Taanis dibbur period of self-imposed silence with the object of self-purification

Tahor pure. See *tamei*

Talmid chacham proficient Talmudic scholar

Tamei impure. A spiritual concept. Adjective of *tum'ah*. Opposite of *tahor*, pure. In Galia's messages, tum'ah mostly implies a state of contamination by the forces of evil. *Tamei* and *tahor* have a further application: In biblical and chazalic belief, the body and many physical items have spiritual integrity. When this integrity is sound, they are described as pure or *tahor*; and when affected, they are described as impure or *tamei*.

Tefillin phylacteries; religious article worn by men during the morning prayers.

Tehillim Psalms. Recitation of Psalms as a form of prayer.

Teshuva return to G-d, repentance; becoming religious

Teshuva sh'layma complete repentance, i.e., rectification of all past sins and evil tendencies

Tikun lit. rectification. In *kabala*, Heaven often sends a soul to the world with a mission to rectify some moral failing it possesses. It might be, for example, throwing temper tantrums, in which case the soul is sent to the world with the object of learning to be calm and accepting. This will be its tikun. If by the time of death, the soul fails to achieve tikun, it may be subjected to a painful process of rectification in the afterworld or sent to earth again for a further attempt (gilgul).

Tikunim plural of *tikun*

Torah she-baal peh the body of the interpretation of the law; the Oral Law

Tum'avv the forces of spiritual impurity; opposite of *tahara*. See *tamei*.

Tzadekes feminine term for *tzadik*

Tzadik one who through painful and self-sacrificing devotion to the letter and spirit of the law has been rewarded by Heaven with a high spiritual level. The level will be commensurate with the *tzadik*'s degree of devotion. There are few perfect *tzadikim*, and numerous levels of *tzidkus*, (the state of being a *tzadik*). In Jewish doctrine, the *tzadik* justifies the world.

Tzadikim plural of *tzadik*

Urim v' tumim in the biblical era, the breast plate of the High Priest, which was made of precious stones with letters engraved upon them. In answer to a question, the letters would light up and convey divine messages. By derivation, an expression to mean the divine seers of our race.

Yetzer hara the evil will. A force inside the person which seeks to lure him to disobey G-d's will. Opposite of *yetzer hatov*.

Yetzer hatov the good will. Opposite of *yetzer hara*.

Yiras shamayim fear of Heaven. A person with *yiras shamayim* can be relied upon to do the will of G-d and does not need external compulsion, such as the threat of punishment.

Zechus merit

Zechus avos merit of the fathers. Refers to children benefiting through the merits of previous generations.

Zechuyos plural of zechus; merits

Zichrona livracha feminine. Of blessed memory.

Zichrono livracha masculine. Of blessed memory.

Zikuy harabim doing an action which leads to the public, or a section of it, gaining merits. For example, in giving a Torah lecture, the lecturer will provide the listeners with the merit of having listened to *divrei Torah*. In parlance, *zikuy harabim* is close in meaning to *kiruv*.

Zohar authoritative book of Jewish mysticism

Zt"l acronym for *zecher tzadik levracha*, "may the memory of the *tzadik* be blessed"